THE MINISTRY OF CLOWNING

Compiled by
EVERETT ROBERTSON

BROADMAN PRESS
Nashville, Tennessee

4275-22
ISBN: 0-8054-7522-2
Dewey Decimal Classification: 791.3
Subject Heading: CLOWNS
Library of Congress Catalog Card Number: 82-71444
Printed in the United States of America

All Scripture quotations are taken from
the King James Version of the Bible.

Introduction

The Ministry of Clowning is the direct result of the surging interest in Christian clowning.

The purpose of the book is to provide a basic how-to manual for Christian clowns. Check the Contents page for areas of special interest.

The book is also the direct result of the efforts of Ernie Liebig, Billy Don Roberts, Bruce Johnson, and Holice Turnbow. These men are extremely talented clowns and are united by one goal: to communicate Christ through clowning.

Each made major contributions to the how-to materials presented in this book. Because each is proficient in all major areas of clowning, I did not want to limit their skills by assigning them a specific area. Thus, they each presented their concepts on clowning and I have compiled their ideas.

Special thanks are also due Jean Liebig, Ernie's wife, for special contributions to the costume chapter. Jean is also an excellent performer. Her puppet character "J. J." adds immensely to Ernie's clowning.

I would also like to thank Tom Rives for his contributions to the Bibliography and makeup chapter. Tom is minister of activities, Red Bank Baptist Church, Chattanooga, Tennessee.

Finally, I would like to thank my wife, Joy, who diligently proofread my writing and continues to be a spring of inspiration.

EVERETT ROBERTSON

A Tribute to the Major Contributors

Ernie Liebig: Nationally known clown and instructor in clowning. Ernie is the executive administrator of the Timberline Baptist Camp and Conference Center, Smith County Baptist Association, Tyler, Texas.

Billy Don Roberts: Nationally known clown and instructor in clowning. Billy is minister of education and youth, Rittenhouse Baptist Church, Houston, Texas.

Bruce Johnson: Nationally known clown and instructor in clowning. Bruce is minister of activities, Immanuel Baptist Church, Lexington, Kentucky.

Holice Turnbow: Nationally known clown and instructor in clowning. Holice is known also as an Adult Sunday School and Church Training conference leader. He is a training officer in the Office of the Secretary, Department of Health and Human Services, Washington, D. C.

CONTENTS

1 Overview: The Ministry Possibilities in Clowning

The Perspective of Clown Ministry

The clown is a universal figure of historical significance. That joyful, sad, elated, frightened enigma is a basic part of all humanity.

Throughout history the clown has been a communication figure presenting the truth of life in exaggerated, fantastic actions.

The clown tears a person from the ignorance of his human condition, pulls him into the spectrum of fantasy, and thrusts him in front of a mirror of life.

This masked, costumed figure has been discovered as a means of bringing the gospel of Jesus Christ to an alienated, hardened, secular world.

Christians are commanded in the New Testament to become "fools for Christ's sake" (1 Cor. 4:10). In other words, the Christian pursues the ideals of Christ even though they may appear foolish to the secular world.

The clown provides a perfect vehicle for the Christian to communicate the truth of the gospel in a way the secular world can comprehend it.

The potential for Christian clowning in outreach is unlimited. The universal nature of the clown also makes it an excellent communication tool to use within the Christian ranks.

The clown is a historically accepted figure in the cultures of the world. Many people in western society identify the clown with the circus. However, traditionally, the clown was an important figure in social life long before the circus appeared.

Slapstick, often grotesque comedians were prevalent in Roman comedy. Later, the clown evolved into a higher character in the *Comedia del Arte*. The court jester was a highly respected member of the court in the Middle Ages.

Universally, the white face is a symbol of death. The markings on the face, however, present life. Therefore, the clown is a figure of life and death.

The rebirth of Christians when they accept Jesus Christ is symbolically represented by a clown's applying makeup and costume. The old character dies, and the clown represents new life. The process of makeup application involves first turning the face white. Later, lines are added.

The clown brings truth through absurd and often ridiculous action. This figure of fantasy presents the foibles of human behavior. We laugh and cry at ourselves through the clown.

Christ used imagination and ingenuity many times to help people understand his truth. Over and over in parables he projected his message through situations involving people and their strengths and weaknesses.

The clown has the potential to make the secular world aware of its predicament and to present Christ as the solution. This potential can only be realized when we discover the best ways to use the clown and then get about the business of putting those ways to work.

First, we must understand more about the clown. Webster's Ninth Collegiate Dictionary defines the clown as "a fool, jester, or comedian in an entertainment (as a play); specifically, a grotesquely dressed comedy performer in a circus. [Also,] one who habitually plays the buffoon."

The clown by its nature is a figure of comedy. However, the clown's comedy does not necessarily invoke laughter from an audience. Sometimes the hard satire is so truthful that an audience may be moved more to tears than laughter.

Great clowns do the unexpected. They present a

basic human action with a problem, and then a solution that appears irrational. For example, one clown might have a squeaky bike seat. Another clown will come along with an oil can and oil every part of the bike except the seat. The first clown must either ride with a squeaky seat, find another means of transportation, or walk. We laugh at the absurdity; yet how true to life that scene really is.

Christians are concerned with presenting Christ, not producing good clowns. Therefore, we must take any element of the clown that can assist us in our goal and use it.

We must never let clowning traditions restrict our ministry. For example, suppose that a Christian clown desires to visit in a children's hospital in character. When the time comes for him to leave, he discovers that his shoes and part of his costume are missing. This should never keep the Christian from his ministry. Even if he had to go with only his face, he can still project joy to those in pain.

Let's consider another example. A Sunday School teacher desires to dress as a clown for a special feature. The teacher has never been a clown or studied clowning. Without question the teacher should use any part of the clown makeup or costume available to assist in ministry.

There are some dangers to be aware of when considering the use of clowning in ministry. A major one is that the clown is a universal communication tool. Therefore, the clown figure can be used for evil purposes as easily as it can be used for the cause of Christ. Every Christian clown and church clown troupe must keep Christ at the center of their ministry.

Be aware of the following gray areas when using clowning with children:

1. Clowns can present the plan of salvation, but they must never extend an invitation to children to make a decision for Christ. The clown is a character of fantasy, but the gospel is very real. The young child may make a decision based on the beautiful clown, not on an understanding of Christ.

2. Never let clowns lead in prayer with young children. Again, the child may associate prayer, which is real, with the clown, which is not.

3. Clowns cannot give a testimony of their character's salvation experience. They are not real and can never be saved. However, the clown can, of course, give his personal testimony. Be certain the child discerns the difference between the clown and his character.

These three concerns are generally problems with young children only. Older children, youth, and adults know that the clown is only a person in costume and makeup.

Clowns can talk or be silent. Traditionally the circus clown talked very little because he could not be heard in a large tent. Historically, however, clowns have always talked. Pantomime by a silent clown can be beautiful.

Floyd Schaeffer, Holice Turnbow, and others who use clowning in worship are silent. Their work is beautiful and certainly worshipful.

Christian clowns should never let silence limit them in ministry. Let's say that a clown has the opportunity to share Christ with a blind person. Which is more important—maintaining the tradition of the silent clown or sharing of Christ?

The most effective clowning will involve a combination of pantomime and speech.

The joyful nature of the clown is attractive in a world of fear and pain. Christ can be projected through that joyful nature in a new and exciting way. Through the clown, lost persons can be presented another opportunity to see Christ and become aware of the saving truth in his gospel.

Four Testimonies of Christian Clowns

The words from the song "Reach Out and Touch" by Charles F. Brown are at the center of my ministry as a Christian clown.

The goal of a Christian clown is to provide an avenue for the Holy Spirit to use in directing and bringing people to a closer personal relationship with Jesus Christ. Clowning is a tool that can be used to minister to the needs of people regardless of their age or the color of their skin.

Why use a clown to minister? Let me share a personal experience with you. In 1979 two other clowns and I went to the Burn Hospital in Galveston, Texas, to visit the children's ward. We went to the playroom of that ward, where we did a makeup demonstration, a magic show, and made balloon animals for the children. Some children, however, could not go to the playroom, so we divided up and went with the nurses to make rounds to these rooms.

Upon entering one of the rooms, I saw a mother crying, so I began to ease back out of the room. Suddenly the mother jumped to her feet and ran to me and began hugging me, saying, "Thank you, thank you, thank you." When the lady calmed down

I asked her why she was thanking me. The lady explained that doctors had told her that her daughter would die unless she snapped out of a deep emotional and mental state. The mother continued, "You see, Mr. Clown, that's the first time my daughter has said a word or laughed out loud in over six weeks. Now there's a new hope."

I reminded the lady to thank God for that new hope. She replied, "Mr. Clown, I don't know him." During the next thirty minutes the lady poured out her heart to me. I began to minister and had the privilege of leading that mother to the Lord Jesus Christ as her personal Savior.

When I got ready to leave the lady said, "You know, I never would have thought a clown could have talked to me that way. I mean. . . ."

I responded, "Yes ma'am, I understand; but remember, I was just a vessel that God chose to use to tell you how much he cares."

Another experience occurred in 1981 when I walked into a Houston home to do a birthday party for a seven-year-old girl. I was greeted by a man who introduced himself as the girl's father. When the little girl and her mother came into the room, there was clearly tension between the father and mother. The little girl was very nervous.

I learned that the man and woman had been separated for almost six months. The father had promised that he would come to his daughter's birthday party. The mother, however, did not like the situation.

I prayed to the Lord to help me minister here in Jesus' name. After a makeup demonstration I went into some presentations of magic.

The closing illustration was the "stratosphere"—a cylinder with three colored balls. I called the balls Faith, Hope, and Love, and used them to illustrate the love chapter from Corinthians.

When I got ready to leave the man said, "I feel like the mule that was hit in the head by a 2 × 4 to get his attention." "Really, how's that?" I responded. He said, "What you did with those colored balls and what you said about love, is that true? How do you know that?"

Talk about getting excited. This was the opportunity I had prayed for.

After the other guests left I sat down and visited with the man and his wife. I shared from God's word the love that he has for us. "Once you experience this love in your life, then you in turn can share it with others," I said. They asked me questions about love's being patient and kind. It was thrilling to be able to relate the forgiveness that comes from knowing the love of Christ.

I asked them if they had ever prayed together and they said, "Well, we go to a Catholic church occasionally."

"Fine. But do you ever pray together?"

"No," they admitted, "we don't."

God allowed me the opportunity to take them step by step to making a commitment for him. They accepted Christ as their personal Savior right there in their living room. Needless to say, we were all crying tears of joy.

The wife looked over at me and said, "No fair."

"What do you mean?" I responded.

"My makeup is running and yours is not," she replied.

We laughed and prayed together again, thanking God for reaching out with his arms of love to meet their needs.

Yes, reach out and touch . . . allowing the love of God to touch and to love through you.

—Billy Don Roberts

My first experience in clowning was one of my most memorable. It occurred over twenty-five years ago and was a very emotional time for me. God's enlightenment in my own heart and life as to the value of clowning occurred at this time. The song "Mr. Custer, I Don't Want to Go" or something like that was popular. My daughter, four at the time, and I were walking in the Rose Parade in Tyler, Texas. I was dressed as Mr. Custer, and she was in a military outfit and sitting on a pony. We both had our faces made up as clowns and wore long boots.

To this day, after all these years, there is an emotional welling that comes up in me when I recall it. I led my little daughter on that pony through the entire parade. There were over 100,000 people present. I cannot describe the impression it made on me as a young adult. The clown portrayal was such a powerful instrument. The people would awe and ooh and then clap and rejoice.

I thought to myself, *Just imagine, here is an ordinary person, who has never been adored in the public eye.* It struck me how powerful the clown can be in the community. I thought to myself, *Here I am; I've given my life to the Lord Jesus Christ, and I go to visit people and tell them about him. But there are so many places where I am rebuffed and turned aside the minute the discussion touches on Jesus.* As I walked along I was filled with emotion when I realized that the clown might be the way to get past those barriers. I immediately started a clown group in our church as a result of that experience.

I don't think it's possible to overestimate the power of the clown in reaching people. For example, several years ago I took six clowns to Monterrey, Mexico, where we worked for a week with the City of Monterrey Orphanage. The orphanage contained 190 boys and girls. It was located about twelve miles outside Monterrey. However, there were nine villages in the area around the orphanage. The director of the orphanage asked us if we could take the clowns and use printed handouts to invite people from the villages to bring their families and come to the orphanage.

We took a few of the older boys and girls from the orphanage and started out. We handed out the tracts and a few lollipops and balloons we had brought with us. We told the people there were going to be free refreshments and there would also be a message for them at the orphanage. We were careful to prepare our actions and words ahead of time since this was a foreign country. We didn't want to do anything to alienate the people.

As we traipsed from one village to another, people began to follow us. As we neared the orphanage and concluded the trek, the television people estimated that there were over two thousand people following us. The line spread over a mile down the road. I remember that the word of God was preached and that three to four hundred people came forward when the invitation was given.

A few clowns with some children led a multitude to hear the gospel. How marvelous it is when we as clowns can bring such crowds to the gospel. The basic fact is that clowns can bring people to the Lord. Clowns draw attention. It was because of the clowns that the multitude gathered that day in Monterrey, Mexico.

I remember the first time I appeared as "Happy" in a worship service. The service was already in progress. I entered, walked down to the front, and said, "Hey, folks, you know Happy is here to let you know that there are some things you don't clown around about. You leave the clowning up to Happy. But some of you folks are clowning around about your life in Christ. You know we are not having any people go out and visit folks. Our visitation on Tuesday night is practically zero. It is the same 12 or 15 people every time. And you know, folks, there ought to be two or three hundred people there on Tuesday night. My, I'm sure our Lord is really ashamed of us because we are clowning around about his business." The following Tuesday night 120 people showed up for visitation.

Several years ago I was standing on a street corner in Houston, Texas, during a Southern Baptist Convention. I was there to promote Church Recreation and to evoke laughter and smiles from the delegates as they passed me. While I was working in the crowd a young couple with an elegantly dressed small child approached me. I was on the street corner giving away lollipops and blowing up balloons.

As the couple approached, the mother mouthed the words that their daughter was blind. I immediately stooped to the level of the child, even though she couldn't see me. Her parents told me her name was Debbie and said, "Debbie, we want you to meet Happy the clown." She became ecstatic. "Oh yes, I do want to meet him." So I said, "I'm so glad that you came to see Happy the clown." Then she said, "Yes, I want to see you." "OK, here, feel my hands."

Then I asked her if she would like to feel my face. "My face is in all kinds of different colors and I have on grease paint. But it won't come off on your hand because it's powdered and you can feel it." I lifted her small hand up to my face and she eagerly felt it. "Would you like to feel my rubber nose?" And she felt the rubber nose. "Now, Debbie, feel my hair. It's a wig, but it makes me look so pretty. It's bright red." She felt all over my wig, smiling all the time. "Now feel my costume." And she did. Then she looked up at her mommy and daddy and said, "You know, Mommy, I see Happy. He is beautiful."

You know, it made me wonder right then and there how many people are told of Jesus our Lord and then even put their hands out and their lives out to touch, but they never feel him and they never see him. Here was this little blind girl able to touch an old clown and get happiness. As she went away she had a little skip in her feet and you could see tears in her mother's and father's eyes as they walked away.

One of the wonderful things about clowning is how many beautiful, out-of-the-ordinary things happen to you. Those parents didn't expect to see a clown. Had I not been there this one little life couldn't have shared the joy Happy was able to give. The ministry is the reason I'm a clown. Happy is the avenue I use to reach people.

—Ernie Liebig

I discovered clowning before God called me to full-time church staff work. I used it many, many ways in recreation centers. When I committed my abilities to the Lord, clowning was included in that. Through the years I've found more and more ways it can be used in the ministry of a church.

Of all the experiences I've had with clowning, one stands out. Several years ago in Kentucky one of our clown groups was waiting to participate in a community parade. A reporter saw our sign from the church and said, "A church with clowns in a parade—why?"

So I said to him: "Aren't we as Christians supposed to laugh and have fun? Or are we supposed to stay inside our churches, playing our solemn music and saying our prayers to God? Jesus said I must be out among my people. He was consistently out; he wasn't in the synagogue. He was out among his people ministering to them, caring for them, loving them, touching them in so many ways." That was one surprised reporter.

I love to watch the reaction of people when they see us (clowns). Their whole attitude changes. People just sort of take off their mask and they begin to laugh. We have the mask of a clown, and they have the mask they wear every day. Even in our churches people wear masks, but theirs don't have makeup. But when people see us, they forget their hurts and laugh with us. They respond in a very positive way.

The clown activities also have a very positive effect on those who are clowning. I remember a man in one of our clown groups who had two teenagers. Both of them were involved in the wrong type of life—alcohol and drugs. That man had a lot of problems. As a person, I don't think he thought much of himself. He worked in the children's area at church and never participated in activities with adults. He was a very quiet person, but he loved children and could relate to them. With adults he couldn't get up in front of two people and speak. But when he put that makeup on, his whole outlook and attitude about life was changed. He became a different person. I've seen him be the spokesman for our group in front of five hundred people. Once at a county fair he got on the PA system and directed our whole routine. Without the makeup and costume, you'd never get him to do anything like that.

Let me share another similar experience with you. We had a young lady with three preschool children in our church. Her husband wasn't a Christian and never attended with her. At home he didn't treat her well—didn't show the respect, love, and care that she deserved. He worked and was gone when he wasn't working—self-centered about his own personal needs and wants. She didn't have a good self-image. When she found out about our clown group she became interested. And when she put on that makeup for the first time, it was one of the best jobs I've ever seen for a person doing it the first time. She was very creative. Because of this her whole personality and attitude changed.

Romans 12:2 says, "And be not conformed to this world: but be ye transformed by the renewing of your mind." I think she was a transformed person. When she was with our group you could tell she felt she was a person of worth. She forgot about herself. The Bible says, "Deny yourself." That's what happened to her. She forgot who she thought she was, and nobody else knew who she was. Because of this she could give freely of herself in care and love for people.

Another time I saw a young man in a high school gymnastic show who could juggle. He was very good at juggling, unicycle riding, jumping on the trampoline, and tumbling. So I contacted him and told him we were trying to start a clown group at our church. He said he was interested and came to our first meeting. It turned out that he was a Christian, but his whole family hadn't gone to church for years. He was a very creative young man and became active in our group. Because of this his whole family eventually joined the church and became very active in its work. Later he assisted a small church in the country (where his grandparents attended) as a volunteer youth director. He started a clown group there and they became very active. That little spark—it takes just a little spark to set the fire going.

We had two young ladies in our deaf ministry who became actively involved with the clown group. Both of the girls could read lips, so we could communicate things to them. There are some routines that they cannot participate in, but there are many other things that they can do. They feel a part of the total work of our church, not just the deaf group.

The clown ministry can offer special opportunities to many people who would not participate in other church activities. It can certainly have a positive effect on the lives of those who participate.

—Bruce Johnson

Our purpose as silent clowns is to go out and show God's love without speaking or any means of written communication. So what do we do? We do what the New Testament tells us to do. We care; we share; we reach out and touch.

The process of being transformed from this world to the world of the clown through costume and makeup is the same process as becoming a "fool for Christ's sake." Our life-style is changed.

The experiences of caring, sharing, and reaching out and touching as a clown have increased my ability to function as a "fool for Christ" in my personal life.

Each day I ride a subway to work. When I exit from the subway I see a flower vendor at work. For many days I thought about who I could give fresh flowers to.

There was a secretary in my office with whom I felt I had developed a strained relationship. One day when I was out to lunch, I passed a flower vendor on the street. Suddenly it occurred to me that I might, like the clown who does the unexpected, take her some flowers. I went to her office, placed the flowers on her desk, turned around, and walked to my office.

When I arrived in my office, the phone was ringing.

"Did you put the flowers on my desk?"

"Yes."

"Did you bring them for me?"

"Yes."

"For what reason?"

"To give you flowers!"

"You don't need anything?"

"No!"

"You don't want any favors?"

"No!"

"Then why?"

"Because I wanted to!"

(Pause)

"Thank you!"

My relationship to that lady has changed dramatically since that moment. I was able to care, to share, and to reach out and touch.

Also in the building where I work, there was a short, neatly dressed lady whom I did not know. She is distinctive in her walk, which can only be described as regal.

Our paths never crossed, but I wanted to express my feelings to this lady.

One day in the cafeteria I noticed that she was sitting alone. I debated what to do. Should I say something? Would it be appropriate?

Finally, I walked over to her table and said, "Hello, my name is Holice Turnbow. We've never met, but I want to tell you that I think you're one of the finest, neatest people I know."

She looked at me and said, "That's the nicest thing anyone has ever said to me. You've made my day. Thank you!"

—Holice Turnbow

Types of Clowns

There are many types of clowns. The major ones are mimes, jesters, white face, auguste, and tramp. Many consider large, full-bodied puppets as actually being clowns. This book will focus primarily on white face, auguste, and tramp clowns. Many techniques of mime and pantomime will be covered, but the application of those will be specifically for the aforementioned figures.

White Face

The white face or "neat" clown is perhaps the best known in the Western culture. This type of clown is a direct descendant of Petrolino in the *Comedia del Arte.* The face is completely white and all areas of the body are covered with makeup or costume. In recent years large mouths and other exaggerated features of the face have been added. Traditionally, however, the white face clown had few markings on the face. White gloves are usually worn, along with large shoes and wigs. The costume is usually of one or two pieces. Often the costume is very large with ruffles at the neck, wrists, and ankles. Colors and decorations are bright and bold. The white face clown deals more with high comedy. The character may speak occasionally or only use mime. Generally the character does not participate in slapstick or in highly physical action.

The Auguste

The auguste clown or "character clown" has evolved primarily during the past one hundred years. Makeup and costume are designed to express a particular type of character. Generally, clothes are very large, bulky, and ill fitting. Colors do not match, and large accessories may be added (pins, buttons, ribbons, etc.). White makeup and other colors cover only parts of the face. Usually the mouth, nose, and eyes are highlighted by exaggerated makeup. The rest of the face receives no makeup. Often gloves are not worn, and there is no attempt to completely cover all parts of the body. For example, shirts may be open at the neck; knee-length pants may be worn with the calves uncovered; even short-sleeved shirts are appropriate.

The auguste clown has grown in popularity in recent years because of the potential for unique character development. Generally large splashes of color are important in costume and makeup. However, as opposed to the white face, certain auguste characters may even be somewhat dark. For example, dark pants and dark shirt might be highlighted with red suspenders, large yellow buttons, and even patches on the pants and shirt.

Traditionally the auguste character has been a low comedian. Action revolves around slapstick action. For example, pratfalls, awkward collisions, large slaps (accompanied by a "whack" sound), and other similar actions are common.

In recent years certain characters have evolved which do not necessarily participate in this slapstick action. Many women prefer auguste characters, but they do not want to participate in the highly physical actions.

The auguste clown may carry a special prop which fits the character. In circuses this prop may be a dog, monkey, or other type of animal. Sometimes it is a puppet. Other special props may include telephones, buzzers, music boxes, umbrellas, horns or other sound makers, wagons with special props, balloons, suitcases, etc. Dolls and even small children may also accompany the character.

Because of props and particularly sound making instruments, the auguste is an excellent walk-around clown. The character works well as an individual or can fit into a group.

The Tramp

Technically, the tramp character is a special character, and hence an auguste clown. However, the great Emmett Kelley so popularized the character that many people began to develop special "tramp" characters. Thus, the tramp has emerged as a major type of clown. Traditionally the tramp is bearded and shabbily dressed with minimal makeup. Also, traditionally the tramp has been the butt of jokes in a clown troupe. For this reason alone, most church groups will find it advantageous to steer clear of the character. It is difficult to find a person with the personality and ability to successfully portray the tramp.

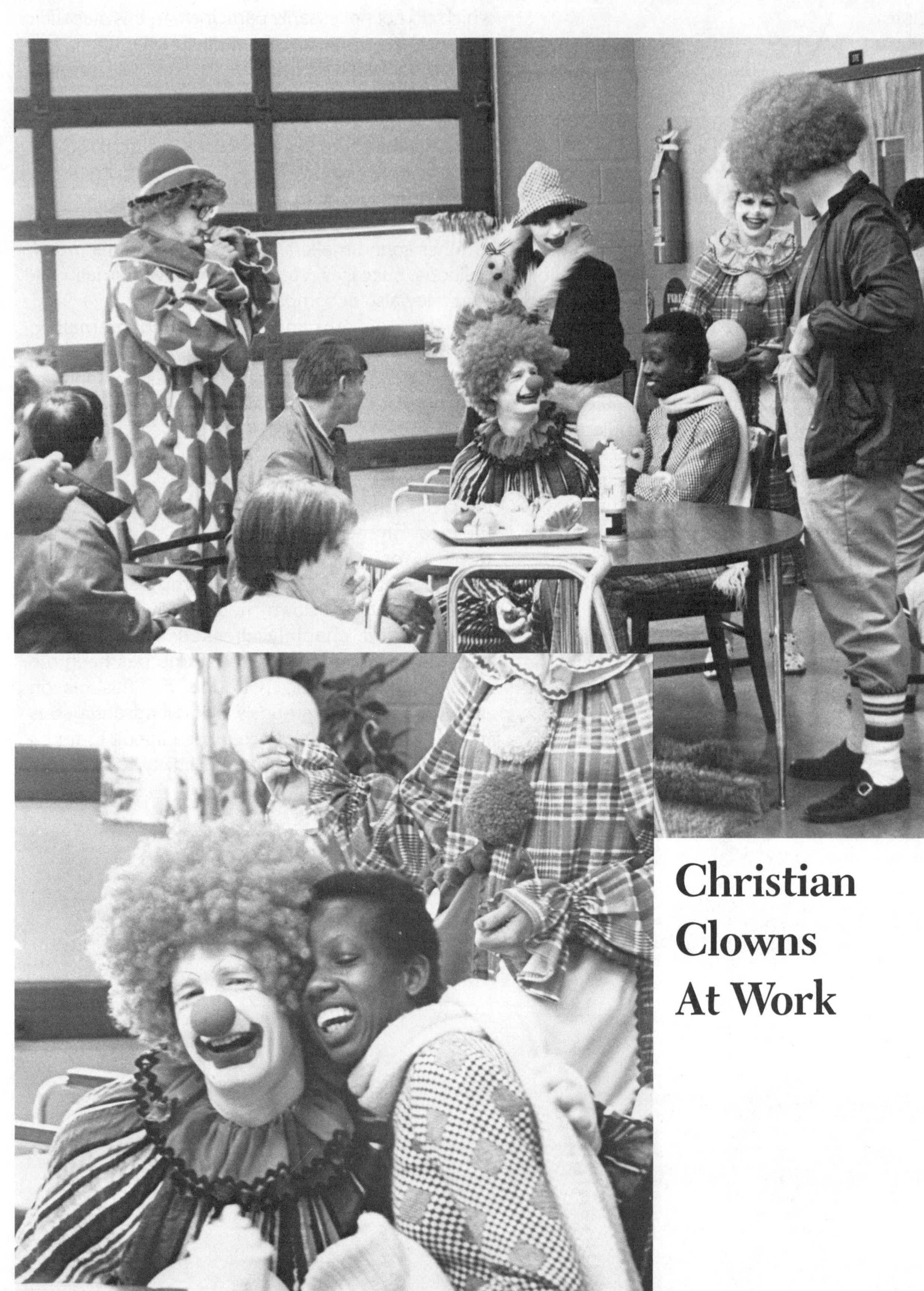

Christian Clowns At Work

THE CLOWN

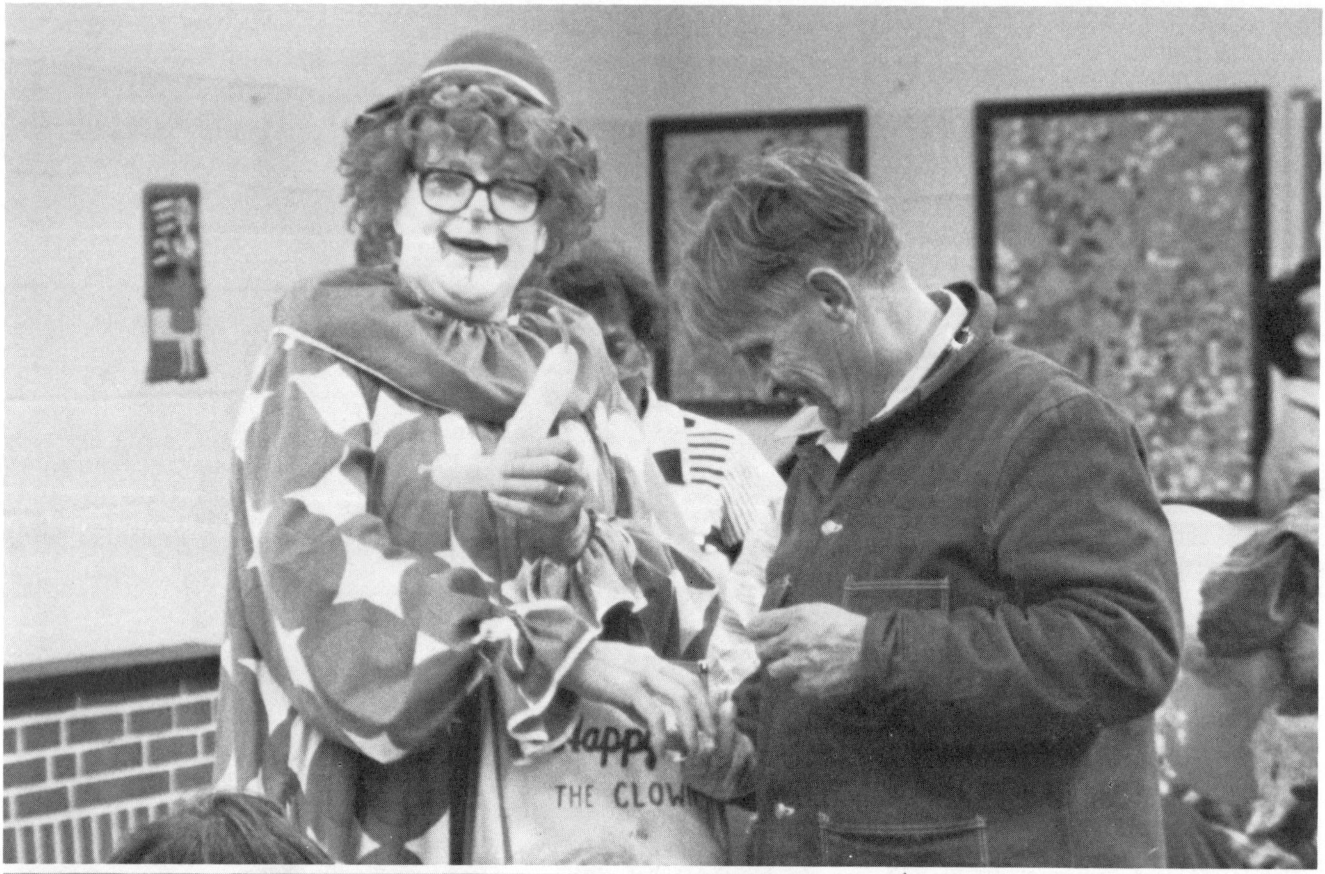

2 Your Church's Clown Ministry

Applications of the Ministry of Clowning

The universal characteristics of the clown provide a resource for use throughout the ministry of a church. Clowning is a proven, valid communication process and can be used in any appropriate setting. Every communication process the church uses is also used in secular life. How the process is used determines its ultimate value in ministry. The same is true with clowning.

An individual clown may be used to promote, educate, entertain, or lead in special worship experiences. Groups of clowns can be used to do the same things. A troupe can do more things than an individual. However, a troupe is rarely as polished or disciplined as a single clown can be. Therefore, be certain to fit the type of clowning to the occasion and audience.

The clown troupe is popular with many churches and is versatile enough for performing many services within the total ministry of a church. The troupe can vary in size from three or four to twenty or more. Generally, break large groups into smaller teams (three to six per team). The large group will perform together sometimes. However, there will be many situations where the small teams will be better suited to the ministry.

Troupes may be composed of youth, adults, or senior adults. As a general rule, avoid using children except for special occasions. The discipline required and physical strain of performing can be difficult for children over a prolonged period. However, there may be special parades or other performances where children can assist.

Some churches build teams around youth. Others mix adults with youth. In recent years several churches have sponsored senior adult troupes. The size of the church and the number of interested persons will ultimately decide the type and size of group.

Organizing for Clown Ministry

The troupe leader is a key to the success of the clown group. This person must be dependable, dedicated, creative, and trained. Clown troupe leaders do not necessarily have to be experienced leaders in the church. Many times, individuals with somewhat limited verbal skills who have not demonstrated leadership qualities may work well with clowning. Amazing transitions can take place when makeup and costume transform the physical appearance. Also, the clown troupe is generally small and becomes very close in their personal relationships. This environment can be an excellent learning experience for the untrained leader who is getting on-the-job training.

The director has the following responsibilities:

(1) Provide spiritual leadership.
(2) Ensure that the troupe objectives coincide with total church ministry objectives.
(3) Oversee the operation of the troupe.
(4) Train and develop personnel to perform as clowns.
(5) Plan and request budget needs.
(6) Schedule and implement performances.
(7) Plan and execute rehearsals.
(8) Assign duties to other members of the troupe.
(9) Lead in the development of routines and other performance material.
(10) Regularly enlist new personnel and provide appropriate training opportunities for these new people.

The first responsibility is perhaps the most important. There are many trained and experienced professional clowns who may not be able to provide spiritual leadership. Without adequate spiritual leadership the clown group can easily slip into activities and pursue objectives that do not meet needs in ministry. The only purpose for the existence of the group is to communicate the gospel. There are, of course, many things that will be outgrowths of this purpose: fellowship, communication skill development, new learning experiences, and many more. However, it is crucial that the director provide spiritual leadership.

An associate director should be enlisted if possible. The associate director has the following responsibilities. If an associate director is not enlisted, then the director must also assume these responsibilities.

(1) Assist the director in the director's ten responsibilities.

(2) Maintain an up-to-date list of names, addresses, and phone numbers of troupe members. Be sure to include work numbers and addresses.

(3) Maintain a performance log. The log should include performance dates and locations. It should also include the sponsoring organization and contact person. Also included are all routines and major props used in the performance.

(4) Notify troupe members in writing (card) or by phone of rehearsals and performances.

(5) Maintain a list of all active routines and skills of individual troupe members.

(6) Oversee storage of makeup, costumes, and props.

(7) Handle transportation, food, and lodging on all trips.

The director, associate director, or a third person should not be in clown costume and makeup for performances. That person(s) drives vehicles and handles logistical matters on trips and in performances. (See chap. 7.)

In addition to the director and associate director, there should be a coordinator for each of the following areas: makeup, costume, and props. These people may all be members of the troupe. However, you may have certain individuals who would like to assist the troupe but do not desire to work in makeup and costume. Assign these individual(s) the above positions.

The makeup coordinator (see chapter on makeup) has the following responsibilities:

(1) Coordinate designs of makeup.

(2) Order all necessary makeup, as budgeted.

(3) Provide storage cases for makeup.

(4) Maintain adequate makeup supplies.

(5) Set up and clean up makeup room and tables.

(6) Train new clowns in makeup techniques.

(7) Carry a travel case with makeup on all trips for emergencies and touch-up.

The costume coordinator (see chapter on costume) has the following responsibilities:

(1) Coordinate costume designs.

(2) Order materials and coordinate construction of costumes.

(3) Purchase costumes and accessories to remain in permanent control of clown ministry.

(4) Store and maintain all costumes.

(5) Select costumes to be checked out to church members who do not participate in the clown troupe.

(6) Check out and see that all costumes are returned in their original condition.

(7) Clean costumes after each performance.

(8) Provide appropriate dressing facilities as necessary.

(9) Care for purses, billfolds, and other personal items while troupe is in makeup and costume.

The props coordinator (see chapter on props) has the following responsibilities:

(1) Coordinate the selection and purchase of all props.

(2) Maintain all props and accessories.

(3) Construct or purchase necessary traveling cases for props.

(4) Handle the storage of props.

(5) Oversee transporting of props on trips.

(6) Work with all clowns in techniques of handling each prop.

Good organization will help ensure smooth operation of the clown ministry. The following suggestions will enhance the value of the clown group to the total ministry of a church. They will also help the organization of the group operate smoothly.

(1) The clown ministry should be represented on the drama committee, recreation committee, or other appropriate church committee.

(2) The clown ministry should be represented in the annual budget of a church.

(3) Enlist leadership at the same time other church leadership positions are filled. Usually this is in the fall of the year.

(4) When possible, train new leaders by having them serve one or more years as associates.

(5) Use the clowns on a regular basis to support other church programs (Sunday School, Church Training, etc.).

(6) Plan major presentations three months in advance. Discuss all presentations with the troupe so they can mark their personal calendars.

(7) Avoid too many performances. Never schedule more than one per week. Two per month is a good average. Individuals may perform more often, depending on interest.

(8) Program the clowns in many different settings. Avoid routine that restricts the group to several performances a year, in the same places, for the same audiences.

(9) Insist that troupe members commit for at least one year of clowning. After that, give them the option to leave the troupe if they wish.

(10) Enlist new clowns every year. Avoid cliques that can form when several clowns make the group a closed society.

Suggested Places to Use Clowns in Ministry

The following list consists of places clowns can be used effectively in ministry. The first group deals with places outside the walls of the church. These are places where people gather. The spirit and gospel of Christ can be carried effectively to these people by the clown.

(1) **Nursing Homes.** Experienced clowns testify that this audience is often the best. They are hungry for visitors, and the clown can bring joy into their dark world. Mix short group performances with plenty of one-on-one work. Remember to circulate to rooms with people who may not be able to move to the performance area.

(2) **Children's Hospitals.** Permission must be obtained from hospital administration to enter. Usually, special performances are not possible. Circulate from room to room in small groups (two or three maximum). You'll find doctors, nurses, technicians, and administrators as receptive as the children. If possible, take balloons or some other item which can be left with the child. Balloon sculptured animals are excellent. Check with nurses before leaving candy and other foodstuffs. Avoid props that are noisy.

(3) **Retirement Homes.** These are excellent places to visit on a regular basis (once a month or once every two months). Plan special performances for each visit. Include plenty of participatory activity for the senior adults. One visit might include making up and dressing interested persons as clowns. When weather permits, move outside for performances.

(4) **Hospitals or Homes for the Mentally Retarded.** Permission must be granted by administrators to enter grounds. Special performances will have little value here. Work primarily one on one. Circulate among patients in small groups of two or three. Candy, balloons, balloon animals, and similar items are excellent to give away. Use a low-keyed approach in prop selection and special sound instruments. Avoid actions or sounds which may excite the patients. Seek to make contact with each individual, but avoid prolonged conversation. Many will try to usurp all your time if they can. Keep moving, and try to project a moment of joy and happiness to each contact.

(5) **Special Olympics Programs for Retarded or Handicapped Children.** Short performances may work if time and space are available. Build actions around physical activity similar to areas they will compete in. For example, rehearse a wheelchair race with two clowns. Use old chairs if possible. The clowns do everything backward, or the opposite of what is expected. They get in the chairs wrong. They race backwards. They end up colliding and never finish the race. Be careful not to mimic the children. However, you can mimic time keepers, starters, audience members, etc.

(6) **Community Parades.** Carry a sign indicating the name of the troupe and the church. Use lightweight props that can be easily carried or clipped to costume. Clown bikes, motorcycles, cars, or instruments to make loud sounds are OK. However, try to do things that are different from other clowns in the parade. Select short routines that project love and joy. Hand out balloons with "Love" on them. You may also wish to hand out small cards that say things such as "Jesus Loves You," "God Loves You," etc.

(7) **Shopping Malls and Streets.** Use walk-around techniques. Props such as telephones, puppets, bells, horns, and fake lollipops (and other similar magic) are excellent. Short two- and three-clown routines can be used. In most cities it's against the law to gather a crowd. Check with local authorities and mall administration for guidelines. Balloons, candy, and cards similar to those suggested for parades will work. Work one on one with

all ages. Pantomime imaginary doors that only they can walk through (see chapter on routines). Coordinate activities with special seasons (Thanksgiving, Christmas, Easter, Labor Day, July 4th) or with special church projects. The clowns can promote revivals, Vacation Bible Schools, day camps, and similar church projects.

(8) **Parks** (national, state, or city). Schedule special performances, fifteen to thirty minutes in length, that will entertain the audience as well as communicate the gospel. Use signs or handouts to promote performances. Also, use walk-around techniques in picnic areas, campgrounds, beaches, and similar places. Coordinate activities with mission agencies or local church as appropriate. The troupe can promote special worship services to be held in the area.

(9) **Special Parties.** These may include birthday, school classroom, Boy Scout, Girl Scout, and similar groups. The troupe plans a special performance that includes routines which present Scripture (see chapter on routines). Check rules and guidelines of the organization and adhere to them. However, always spend a moment telling the group who you are and what church you represent, and invite them to attend.

(10) **Civic Organizations.** Volunteer to assist organizations such as the Jaycees, Kiwanis, and similar groups. These groups have many public service activities that the troupe can assist in.

Consider taking the troupe anyplace where people gather. In addition to the above places, consider sporting events, state and county fairs, public recreation areas, special concerts, prisons, public transportation stations, special cable television programs, and festivals.

Many communities now have small cable television stations with little or no local programming. Coordinate clowning, puppetry, and drama in special Saturday morning features. Develop special themes in these sessions, or introduce Bible study material for Sunday. These stations may have only one camera, but a live presentation can be very effective if carefully rehearsed. Consider renting or purchasing videotape equipment to shoot your own programs. Then provide local stations with the videotape for free public information broadcast.

The second list of suggested places to use the clown troupe deals with situations inside the walls of the church.

(1) **Fellowships, Parties, Banquets.** The entertainment value of the clown is natural for these environments. Use planned and rehearsed programs. Involve audience response when possible (see chapter on routines). Act out improvised scenes of activities in the church. Example: Pantomime the choir singing, using exaggerated actions. Or select other situations appropriate for the fellowship. End the performance by circulating through the group if time permits. Speak to individuals, hand out balloons, help ladies from their seats, etc.

(2) **Promotion.** Use the troupe or individual members of the troupe to promote special programs and activities. This may be accomplished in worship services, Sunday School, training programs, men and women's organization meetings, or wherever members gather. Consider using the clowns at doors on Sunday morning to hand out promotional materials as members enter the church. Improvised scenes can be developed. Special signs can be carried. The clowns will definitely call attention to the item being promoted.

(3) **Sunday School.** The clown troupe or individuals in the group can introduce lesson material in opening assemblies. Example: If the lesson deals with stewardship, have the clowns enter and pantomime the widow and her mite, or a modern parallel to the biblical parable. A clown might also present a worship feature during the opening assembly ("The Rose" or a similar routine: see chapter on routines). The clowns can improvise situations designed to inspire members to bring friends to Bible study.

(4) **Organizational Meetings.** Clowns can introduce study materials for children and youth, as well as adult church organizational meetings. One or more clowns can visually present special problems to be considered by a special committee. The troupe can highlight projects the organization is involved with.

(5) **Training Sessions.** Clowns can assist in training projects by visually presenting problems. Example: the clowns could act out how not to visit, doing each action wrong. Or the clowns could present an exaggerated improvisation of the problem being probed. The exaggerated actions would emphasize the necessary procedures to be followed. The very presence of clowns adds a new dimension to the meeting. However, be sure to use the troupe in some meaningful action, or they may be distracting to the purpose of the meeting.

(6) **Special Worship Experiences.** The joy of worship is happy, not sad. Clowns have had success in leading special worship periods that focus on the joy of worship (see worship section in routines). Some pastors have even used clown techniques for special Lord's Supper presentations. Be careful that actions of the clowns could not be misinterpreted. Prepare the audience ahead of time for the clowns. Explain symbolic meanings so that when the clowns begin, the congregation is prepared to follow their leadership in worship.

(7) **Camps, Retreats.** Clowns add a special dimension to these meetings. Clowns are particularly effective on retreats. The clown aids in the escape from problems of everyday life. Clowns can be effective in leading sharing sessions and worship periods, as well as fun times. One clown group made up participants at the retreat. Each clown made up the face of a participant to express the inner feelings of the participant. A relaxed, open atmosphere was the result.

(8) **Vacation Bible Schools.** A basic purpose of clowns in VBS is to build attendance. Clowns can be promoted as going to be present. On enrollment day clowns can perform and generally entertain. They can ride clown bicycles, use rope tricks, flower tricks, make balloon sculpture, hand out candy, etc. Then each day the clowns can make special presentations during refreshment periods. Or they can entertain participants at the conclusion of each day's activities. Clowns have been used successfully to present special Scripture readings each day. Clowns can also be used to assist in reporting to the church what was accomplished in VBS.

Clowns can certainly be used successfully in any church program or activity. However, remember that they can also be overused. Any communication tool which is used repeatedly will become old and eventually boring. Let the clowns be a fresh addition to a program, not a boring interlude. The clown troupe must be careful to keep each routine and activity fresh and new.

Beginning a Clown Ministry

How the clown troupe begins will depend on the number of people interested and the financial resources available. Survey the church membership to find interested persons. Or advertise in the church paper, by posters, or with announcements that such a group is being started.

The initial announcement may or may not have broad response. A small response can be handled in two ways. (1) Begin the troupe with only the interested persons, perhaps two or three. (2) Personally enlist people who are not overloaded with other church responsibilities. Successful groups can result from either of these two beginnings.

Organize immediately by at least selecting a director. If the group is small, assign other responsibilities to the team members.

Most churches prefer to avoid tryouts or auditions. These can be frustrating for participants and give a negative connotation to those not selected. Remember that the best clowns are often people who give no outward sign of clown skills. They come to life when they put on makeup and costume, and a character is developed.

Plan a special training period for the initial start of the group. This might be a retreat (weekend), two or three Saturday sessions, or several weeknights in succession. This training period needs to be intensive and over a short period of time. The retreat is the best if it can be scheduled.

During the initial training period pursue the following training. (1) Study the overall objectives of the ministry and how it will function. (2) Study the various types of clowns. (3) Study basic clowning techniques. (4) Begin individual character development for each clown (see chapter on character development). (5) Begin experimenting with makeup and faces for each clown. (6) Discuss various types of costumes and which one is most appropriate for the character being developed. (7) Start developing special skills for each character. Examples: juggling, mime, balloon sculpture, rope tricks, simple magic, musical instruments, etc. (8) Develop some initial simple routines involving all members of the troupe. (9) Discuss the construction or purchase of special props. Examples: clown bikes, unicycles, flash boxes, etc. (10) Spend time building spiritual strength in the group. Clown troupes tend to become close-knit groups. Begin at the start with sharing sessions, prayer times, and devotionals.

Next, establish regular meeting times. This may be once a week, once every two weeks, or whatever is practical. However, if the troupe is going to work year-round, rehearsals need to be regular.

Schedule a performance as soon as is practical. The first performance should take place during the first month of operation if possible. Nothing will kill the spirit of a troupe quicker than week after week of rehearsals and meetings and no performances. Clowns learn by doing.

The first performance should be for a small audience, preferably a church group. In fact, the first few performances should be in the church. This will give the troupe time to refine makeup, become acquainted with audience response, develop performance skills, and learn to work together.

After two or three months, or four or five performances, plan a trip outside the church. Retirement homes are a good place to start. The group needs five or six months of experience before moving into the streets (malls, parades, etc.). Remember that in those settings the troupe must be very professional. The secular audience will judge you initially on what you do and how well you do it. Amateurish blunderings that bring comments such as, "Must be some little church group. They ought to stick to preaching," can actually be a negative factor in witnessing.

Rehearsals

The number and length of rehearsals will depend on the participants and the time they can commit. Generally a short fifty-minute to one-hour meeting a week is better than one four- or five-hour session per month.

The director and associate director plan the rehearsal. During each rehearsal, schedule the following activities:

(1) Group sharing, prayer, and devotional time.
(2) Individual skill development.
(3) Improvise new routines.
(4) Review and rehearse old routines.
(5) Work with individual and group mime.
(6) Become acquainted with new props and equipment.
(7) Repair damaged props and costumes if time permits.
(8) Plan upcoming performances.
(9) Run through each part of the next performance.
(10) Review the calendar of coming performances.

The rehearsal should be planned with as much variety built in as possible. Avoid spending the entire rehearsal on one routine. Allot every activity a time slot and stick to it. Initially, this may be difficult, but in time the director will know how much time it takes the group to work on any one activity.

Sample Rehearsal Schedule

7:00-7:10	Sharing, prayer, and devotional. Led by Andy.
7:10-7:15	Individual and group pantomime (with or without music).
7:15-7:20	Review one or more group routines.
7:20-7:25	Plan order of activities for next performance.
7:25-7:35	Improvise one or more new routines.
7:35-7:45	Walk through the next performance.
7:45-8:00	Individual skill development.
8:00	Review calendar and dismiss.

The key to successful rehearsals is preparation by the director. For example, planning an order of activities for the next performance could take a long time if the director is unprepared. However, if the director has thought through two or three tentative plans, the group can simply select one. Improvising new routines also requires preparation. The director needs to have some general ideas in mind (see chapter on routines).

The associate director needs to contact everyone and inform them of the rehearsal. If certain members must miss, the rehearsal schedule can be altered so time will not be wasted. The associate director needs to set up all props, sound equipment, and other special items to be used in the rehearsal. These should be in place and ready when the rehearsal begins.

Usually, costume and makeup are not worn in rehearsals. However, it may be advantageous to provide old costumes for beginning clowns. This will help them get used to moving around in costume.

Large groups, eight to ten or more, may need to be divided into small teams for improvising new routines. Be certain that adequate leadership is available for each team. Each team should rehearse in a different room if possible.

Adding New Members to the Troupe

During the early weeks of troupe development, avoid continually adding new people. This will interrupt the development of the troupe. It is essential that the troupe obtain a high level of proficiency as soon as possible.

Select certain periods during the year when new people will be added. In many cases this may be once a year. Large troupes with trained and skilled leaders may be able to add new members more often.

The director, associate director, or another member of the troupe is assigned the job of orientation and training for each new member. It is certainly more efficient if several can be trained at once.

It may be possible to begin new troupes on a regular basis. However, as a general rule, the new clowns will learn quicker if they can serve as apprentices in a group that is already trained and experienced.

Schedule one or more retreats for the troupe annually. During the retreat provide orientation and training for new troupe members. Use the retreat as a time to regroup and develop new skills for the older members of the troupe.

Beginning a clown troupe can be an exciting experience. The process just described is a general one. You may need to make some changes and alterations to get your group off the ground. Every clown troupe is different. It's very important that your troupe meet the needs of your church and your community. Do whatever is necessary to ensure that the troupe supports the ministry of your church in your community.

3 Choosing a Clown Character and Personality

Character Development

"Exciting clowns," "beautiful clowns," and "joyful clowns" are terms often used to describe good clown troupes. One of the keys to successful clowning troupes is a variety of clown characters. These characters are highly developed and consistent. Professional clowns may have one character all their lives. Occasionally they will change characters during their lives, but each is highly developed and refined.

The ministry value of church clown troupes will be greatly increased when characters are highly developed and consistent. The joy of Christ projected by the clown character will have even greater meaning as the character develops.

This chapter deals with the process of developing clown character. The process will vary from clown to clown; however, the following discussion is intended to provide some guidelines to assist in that development.

Meaningful clowning depends on a thorough understanding of who a clown is and what he does. Review chapter 1 for more information.

Clowns present an exaggerated mirror of life. Christian clowns claim as their purpose the projection of Christ through their clowning. In other words, they present an enlarged and exaggerated mirror of Christ and Christian life.

Clowns often help us see the truth by distorting the truth. Through the distortion we understand.

Traditionally, the clown does what we least expect. He surprises us with a solution to a simple problem. One of the techniques used is to do the opposite of what is expected. For example, one bucket is full of water and the other is empty. The action calls for pouring water from the full bucket into the empty one. The easiest way to do that is to pick up the bucket and pour from it. The clown may take a completely different approach. He might bring a spoon and dip water one spoonful at a time into the empty bucket. Or he might do the same thing with a cup. Or he might take the full bucket and pour the water on the ground instead of pouring it into the empty bucket.

By the above actions the clown shows us how we make the easiest jobs difficult. The symbolic meaning of the clown's action speaks to us with a new truth. Every action by every clown should carry symbols. The clown himself is a symbol (see chap. 1).

In the above illustration the clown should eventually succeed in getting the water from one bucket to another. If the water has been thrown on the ground, he may have to dig up the ground and shovel it into the bucket. The possibilities are unlimited. The actions selected by the clown should be consistent with character.

Discovering Your Character

Developing character is the process of discovering the clown inside of you. The purpose is to strip away self until the character emerges. One of the ways of doing this is to improvise many different and seemingly unrelated actions. The more actions that are carried out, the more elements of character that will begin to emerge.

The following list includes fifty suggested actions. Take time to develop the actions you select to do. Begin with the large, full-body actions. Don't spend a lot of time planning the action. Simply begin. If you don't like the way you're doing the action, then change.

For example: The first action is pushing a large rock. The rock is imaginary, and the possibilities for moving it are unlimited. Some may shove it with a shoulder. Others may push it with their feet. Others may try to pull it. Some may try to wedge a board under it. Another person may tie a rope around it and try to pull the rope. The key is not to think about the action, but to do it.

Try some of the suggested actions. Mix actions which you initiate, i.e. moving the rock, with actions that you must react to (rain, snow, etc.). How you react to each action carries the true meaning of the action to the audience. All physical items are imaginary.

1. Pushing a large rock.
2. Lifting barbells or heavy weights.
3. Pulling a heavy sled.
4. Reacting to a strong wind.
5. Reacting to a sudden rain.
6. Reacting to cold wind and snow.
7. Crossing a ditch with water (or without water).
8. Crossing a busy street.
9. Planting a flower.
10. Picking a flower.
11. Greeting and waving to a child.
12. Hitching a ride.
13. Driving a car.
14. Driving a big truck or bus.
15. Carrying sacks of groceries for a lady.
16. Mopping the floor.
17. Changing a tire.
18. Blowing up a balloon.
19. Blowing out candles.
20. Eating a hamburger.
21. Eating a steak.
22. Eating spaghetti.
23. Eating hot soup.
24. Standing in a long line in summer.
25. Stacking large boxes or crates.
26. Washing windows.
27. Washing, polishing, and/or shining a car.
28. Painting a wall.
29. Walking on stickers.
30. Picking and eating an apple.
31. Picking and eating a banana.
32. Digging a deep hole.
33. Shining shoes.
34. Brushing dirt from another clown's suit.
35. Building a fire.
36. Tossing a baseball.
37. Hitting a baseball.
38. Hitting a golfball.
39. Putting a golfball.
40. Diving in a swimming pool and swimming.
41. Kicking a football.
42. Passing a football.
43. Sitting on a crowded bus.
44. Cheering at a football game.
45. Directing traffic at an intersection.
46. Walking a dog.
47. Swatting a fly or other insect.
48. Taking out the garbage.
49. Dusting furniture.
50. Jogging.

Most of the above actions could easily be expanded into routines. Improvise with each. Let your imagination carry you into the world of the action. Have other members of the clown troupe watch you. Let them judge your consistency in handling actions. Ask them what they see when you pantomime. Beginning clowns will discover that sometimes they are approaching an action one way, but the audience will judge it entirely differently. Simplicity in execution is the key.

Some of the above actions call for words, but most can be expressed silently. Act out the silent actions first. Add words only after character has begun to emerge.

After working one on one with the above actions, involve the entire troupe in one action. Let everyone shine the same car. Notice the great variety in how the clowns carry out their actions.

Sometimes selected group activity by the entire clown troupe can help character emerge. The following are some actions that might be improvised by the entire troupe. All objects are imaginary.

1. Group in a circle tossing a volleyball.
2. Group in a circle tossing a baseball.
3. Group playing baseball with imaginary ball and bat.
4. Group playing volleyball with imaginary ball and net.
5. Group stacking sandbags.
6. Setting up tables for a banquet.
7. Loading furniture onto a van.
8. Digging a long ditch.
9. Building a bonfire.
10. Searching for Easter eggs.
11. Decorating a Christmas tree.
12. Eating at a cafeteria.
13. Playing at an amusement park.
14. Fishing on a pleasure boat.

15. Raking leaves.
16. Putting out a fire.
17. Painting a house.
18. Watching a football game.
19. Picking and loading apples on a truck.
20. Playing tug-of-war.

Selecting a Clown Face

The clown face is the central point of focus of the character. All other physical elements stem from the face. Clown characters evolve, and the makeup for the characters will also evolve. However, the clown must start with some type of face (see chapter on makeup for details).

Initially, the beginning clown can study other clown faces. Never copy another clown's face, however; that face may inspire you to develop a particular look and character. Look through clown and circus books. Study magazines with clown pictures. Watch for subtle touches in professional clown makeup.

Next, begin a study of structure, lines, and textures of people's faces. Study many types of people. Look carefully at people you know. Look closely at pictures in books. Notice particularly the shape of the face and the overall expression of the face.

Select clown faces and human faces that you like. Gradually eliminate the faces until you have three that you really like. Then begin the process of making up your own face.

After you have learned to apply the makeup, work to make the face as expressive as possible. Study your own face. The mouth, eyes, and nose are the facial features most often exaggerated by clown makeup. What type of face will fit your character? Joyful? Happy? Sad? Playful? What size must the mouth be? What size the eyes? The nose?

When these questions are answered, you will have a face that is initially expressive of the character. Remember that your makeup will evolve, so each time you apply it, try to make it as expressive as possible.

The final step is to refine and simplify the face. Many people put too much detail into clown face makeup. Many lines, stars, dots, etc. can be visually confusing and distract from the true expression of the face. Simplify as much as possible.

Selecting a Costume

Think of the costume as clothes for the character. At this point the character has begun to be developed and a face has been selected. Now, simply dress the character. What type of clown are you? White face or auguste? Select a costume that is consistent with the style of clown you are.

What type of design best suits the character? Bright colors? Dull checks? Strong solids? Faded colors? The possibilities are unlimited. If you can't make up your mind, talk to an experienced clown about your character. Let him or her make costume suggestions.

Auguste clowns may find their costumes piece by piece at used clothing stores, garage sales, and similar places. The character will need more than one suit of clothes. Different clothes fit different occasions.

One costume may be very dressy for special performances. Another may be very bright for parades and similar activities that are viewed from a distance. Others may be primarily comfortable for all-day events.

The costume and accessories may be constructed (see chapter on costumes). This is the best direction to go if possible. The clown can completely control color, line, and expression in the costume.

Accessories are very important to the complete physical expression of the character. The following are a few of the accessories to be considered: wigs, hats, buttons, pins, ruffles, patches, gloves, and shoes. (For a complete listing, see chapter on costumes.)

Now, the visual expression of the character is complete. The next step is to project the character to an audience. What does the character do? How does he do it? Look for special skills and activities for your character.

Special Character Skills

Great clowns are remembered for what they do and how they do it. The more versatile the skills of the clown, the more effective the clown in ministry. Professional clowns often spend all their time discovering one unique thing they can do and then refining it. This limits the expression of the character.

Most church troupes will find it advantageous to have characters as flexible as possible. Every character should learn some juggling, clown magic, and mime techniques. Each should also be adept at tumbling, stage falls, balloon sculpture, handling puppets, and other props (see chapter on props).

It is not so much what the character does but how he does it that is important. How the character juggles, how the character falls, and how the character mimes are all important.

As the beginning clown learns special skills, express those skills through the character. One character may like to juggle oranges, another apples. What is juggled becomes as important as how it is juggled.

Spend whatever time it takes to learn to execute these skills flawlessly. Clown magic tricks require just as much precision as a magician. A sloppy trick takes away the power of the character's expression.

Special props may also be used for the character. One character may always carry an umbrella. Another always has a puppet. Another character may carry a horn, another a cow bell, another a battery-run guitar.

Hopefully the character carries the appropriate prop for the occasion. For example, it's difficult to do balloon sculpture while moving in a parade. Select something else. If you feel your character should always carry an umbrella, then carry one. However, this will limit what the character can do in certain situations. It's basic in the philosophy of Christian clowning to be willing to sacrifice elements of the clown for the sake of ministry (see chap. 1).

Experience will bring the character, makeup, costume, and action into one complete, powerful expression. The more varied the experiences, the better the clown. Look for new experiences for your character to express himself.

Exercises

The following exercises are designed to help the clown be as versatile and powerful a communicator as possible. Some of the exercises will be good warm-ups before a performance. Others are designed to develop muscles and special performance skills.

Warm-up Exercises

1. Stretch for the ceiling with arms and on toes. Then collapse from the waist and let upper torso dangle.
2. Shake the hands as if wringing them.
3. Shake the legs one at a time.
4. Shake each arm from the shoulder.
5. Drop the head forward and rotate between the shoulders.
6. Bend from the waist backward as far as possible.
7. Bend from the waist forward and to the sides.
8. Touch the toes, squat, then stand.
9. Shake all the body at once.
10. Jump and land on all fours.

Spatial Awareness Exercises

These are designed to assist the clown in mime work. They will also help in the total physical expression of the character.

1. Walk through imaginary fluids. Imagine you are in the bottom of a swimming pool filled with water or other fluids. Push through the fluids as you walk.

2. Arm movements in fluids. Imagine the arm is being pulled up by a string attached to the wrist. Move the arms accordingly.

3. Push imaginary walls. Imagine you are standing by a wall. Place your hand against the wall and begin to push it back. Imagine the wall is different sizes and weights. Repeat the exercise.

4. Toss imaginary objects. Toss an imaginary baseball in slow motion. Imagine you are tossing the ball through fluids. Use the entire body in the movement. Practice with both arms and different objects.

5. Speed control exercises. Select some actions and practice at different speeds: slow motion, slow, normal, fast, double time. Identify each of the speeds in your mind and remember how they feel.

Exaggeration Exercises

These exercises are accomplished by selecting various actions and making them enormous in expression.

1. Toss an imaginary ball. Then make the gesture twice as large. Continue expanding it as much as possible.

2. Take several normal steps. Then double the size of the steps and continue the expansion.

3. Wave the hand. Then double the size of the wave and continue the expansion.

4. Shake hands with an imaginary person and then expand the action.

5. Pantomime gestures of eating and expand them.

Interaction with Other Clowns

These are basic actions clowns will use from time to time. Rehearse these together. Remember, the key to success is not so much the action as the reaction to the action. For example: A clown is kicked by another clown. The kicked clown may jump several feet forward, fall down and roll over three or four times. Again, exaggerated action is the key.

1. **Slaps.** Rehearse slaps on the back, shoulder, and face. Use a "slap" sound and coordinate it with the action. This can be accomplished by percussion instruments or by another clown turning his back to the audience and clapping his hands.

2. **Kicks.** One clown kicks another clown, but the recipient should not feel the kick. The kick and the reaction by the recipient blend into one smooth action. Coordinate the "slap" sound with the action.

3. **Trips.** One clown trips another clown. The tripped clown executes a stage fall and bounces immediately up. Sound effects coordinated with the action will add to it.

4. **Shoves.** One clown shoves another clown from the front, back, or side. The recipient reacts by running several feet and finally stopping or falling. The shove and the reaction should be done at the same speed and blend into one movement.

Note: The above actions should blend into the appropriate routine. They should never call attention to themselves or look out of place. They are always caused by dramatic action in the routine.

Tumbling

A few tumbling techniques will be handy skills for all clowns. Older clowns may draw the line here, but youth and young adults should develop some of these skills.

1. **Somersaults.** Practice forward and backward somersaults. Practice on mats or extra thick carpet.

2. **Leaps, Jumps.** Practice running jumps, moving the feet double time while in the air. Practice the same technique from a standing position.

3. **Cartwheels.** Stretch the body straight. Try to keep the legs the same distance apart that the arms are.

4. **Leapfrog Jumps.** Practice leapfrogging over each other. One clown bends forward from the waist with hands on knees. Another clown jumps over him from the rear. The jumping clown places hands on the back and springs over.

Vocal Exercises

Strong, well-projected vocal sounds add a powerful dimension to the clown troupe.

1. **Projecting Sounds.** Practice tossing words or sounds over an imaginary fence at the rear of an auditorium or large room. Do not yell. Simply *toss* the sounds over that fence.

2. **Expanding Words.** The way the clown expresses himself vocally is as important as what he says. For example: Ouch might become Ouuuuuuuuuuuuuuuuch, with the *ch* sound being very quick. Another example: Heeeeeeeeeeeeeeeeeeeeelp or You Get Ouuuuuuuuuuuuuut. A good exit line is: I'm Goinnnnnnnnnnnnnnnnnnnnnnnng (said as the character exits and carried offstage).

3. **Rehearse special sounds that can be made with the mouth:** whistling, horses galloping, water dripping, Donald Duck voice, motor boats, car shifting gears, etc.

Flawless execution of these suggested actions and sounds adds a professional dimension to the clown performance. However, these techniques must be rehearsed over and over until they are almost perfect in performance. Then and only then will the characters spring to life in an exciting and meaningful way for the audience. Clowning requires physical action, and these actions must be well executed and well rehearsed. The clown must stay in top physical condition to execute them well.

Pantomime Techniques

Pantomime has traditionally been an important part of clown expression. In circuses, before amplified sound was possible, clowns simply could not be heard. So they depended on physical action to communicate to the audience.

Pantomime remains popular today because some ideas are expressed better with actions than words. For example, a clown saying "I love you" with clean, pantomimed gestures can be much stronger than the verbal statement of the phrase.

Gesture is a universal language. Pantomime is therefore instinctive in all of us. Everyone can express himself to some extent through gesture. However, projecting that expression for an audience requires technique.

Most clown pantomime deals with the expansion and exaggeration of realistic action. Often props are involved with the pantomime. At other times the props will be imaginary. Recorded music or live sound effects are often used.

Successful pantomime depends on clean, precise gesture that is easily understood by the audience. To accomplish this, the beginning clown should follow these guidelines.

1. Slow the action down in performance from what would be normal or regular speed. This helps the clown execute cleanly and also helps the audience follow the movements. The greater the distance between clown and audience, the slower the action.

2. Accomplish one action at a time. Concentrate on each action and keep it as simple and clean as possible.

3. Always lead with the eyes. Let the eyes tell the audience where the action is going. Example: Let's say the clown is picking a flower. (a) Look at the flower, real or imaginary. (b) Move to the flower. (c) Bend to the flower. (d) Reach for the flower. (e) Pluck the flower in one smooth action. (f) Stand. (g) Smell the flower. (h) Look at a person. (i) Move to that person. (j) Hand him the flower. During this action the clown's eyes are focused first on the flower and then on the person. The eyes should not look anywhere else or break the concentration on the action.

4. Emotion is an important part of every pantomime. How does the clown feel when he is picking the flower? Is he eager? Or does the beauty of the flower and the reason for picking the flower cause him to move slower, almost as if he is in awe of the flower? How does he feel when he gives the flower to a person? These questions are answered by how the actions are executed. Every action has some accompanying emotion.

5. Express every action with the complete body. Commit every muscle to the action. This is not easy to do and will require concentration and practice.

As a general rule, keep pantomimes short and simple. Powerful communication is the result of how something is presented, not necessarily what is presented.

1

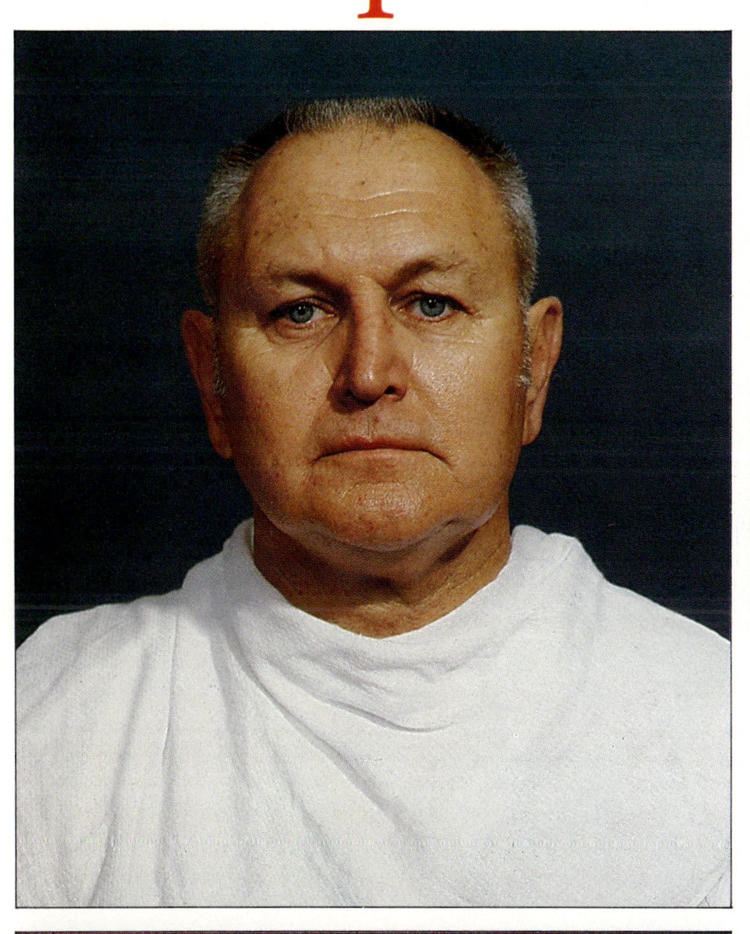

2

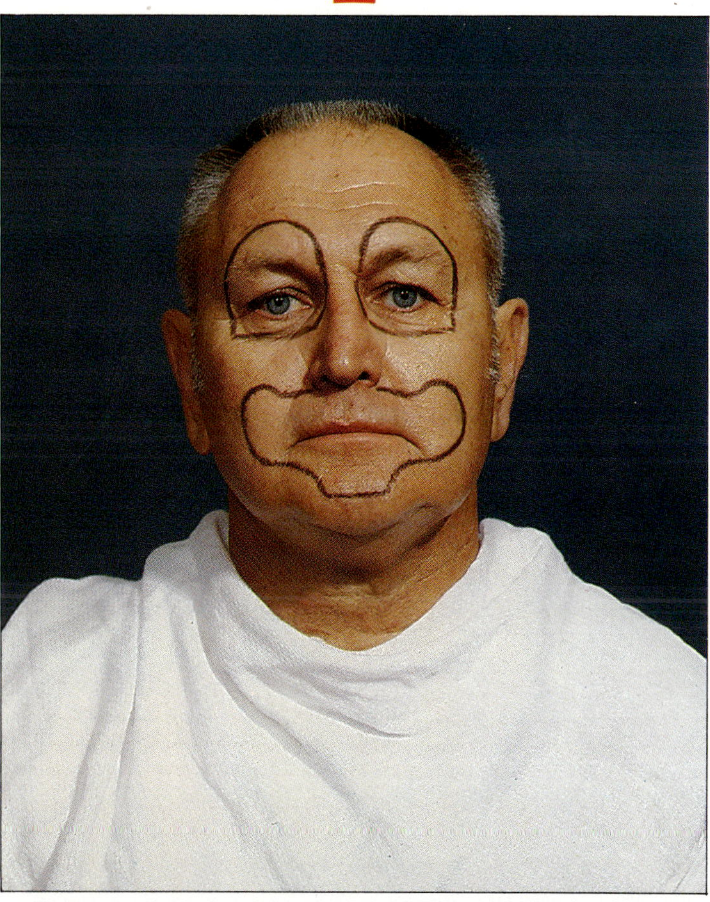

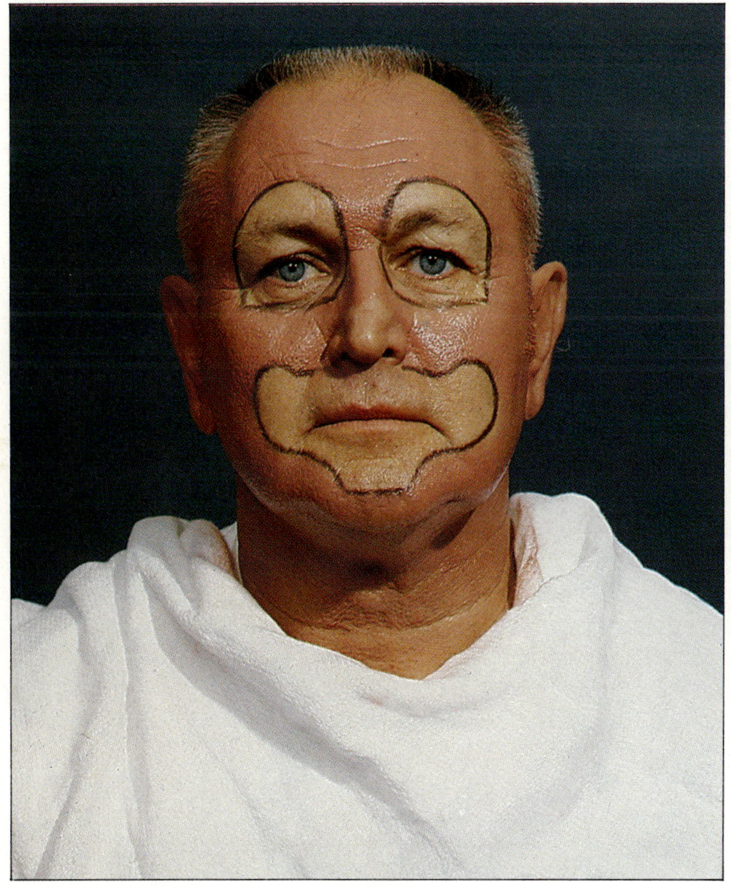

3

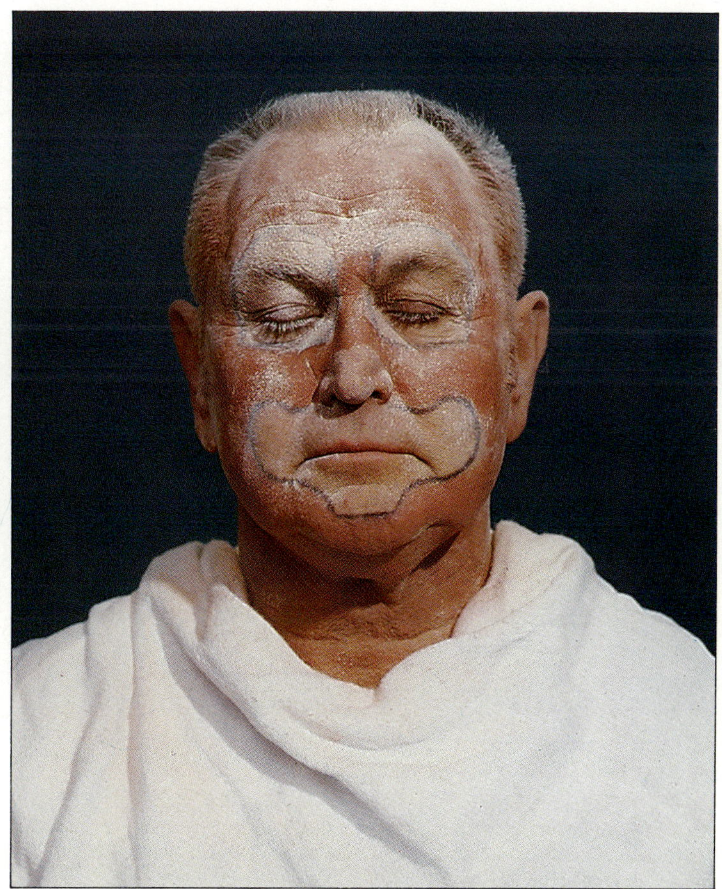

4

5

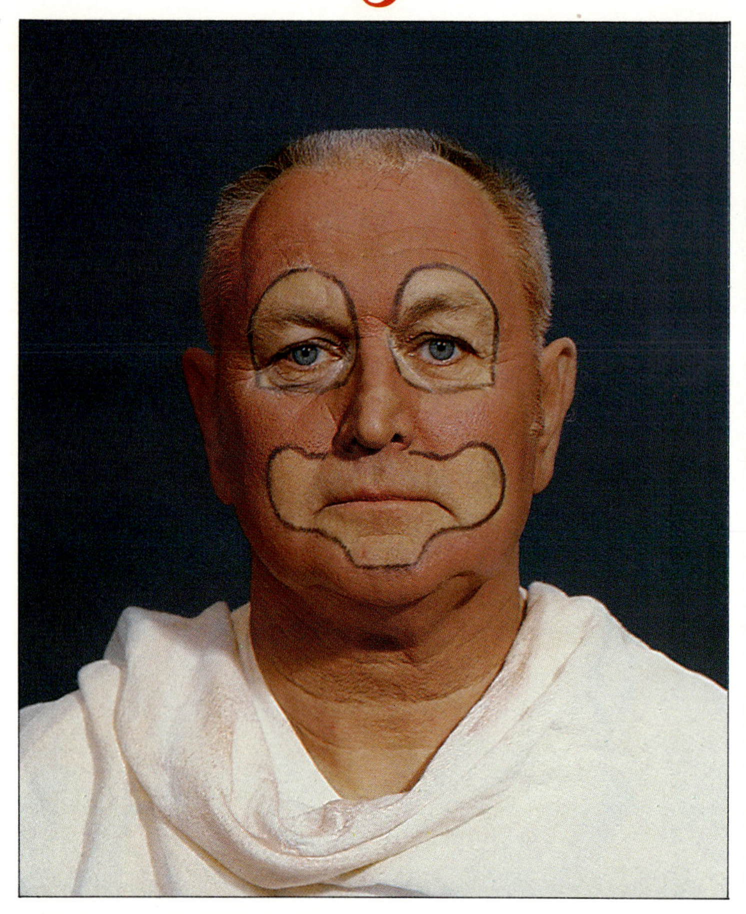

6

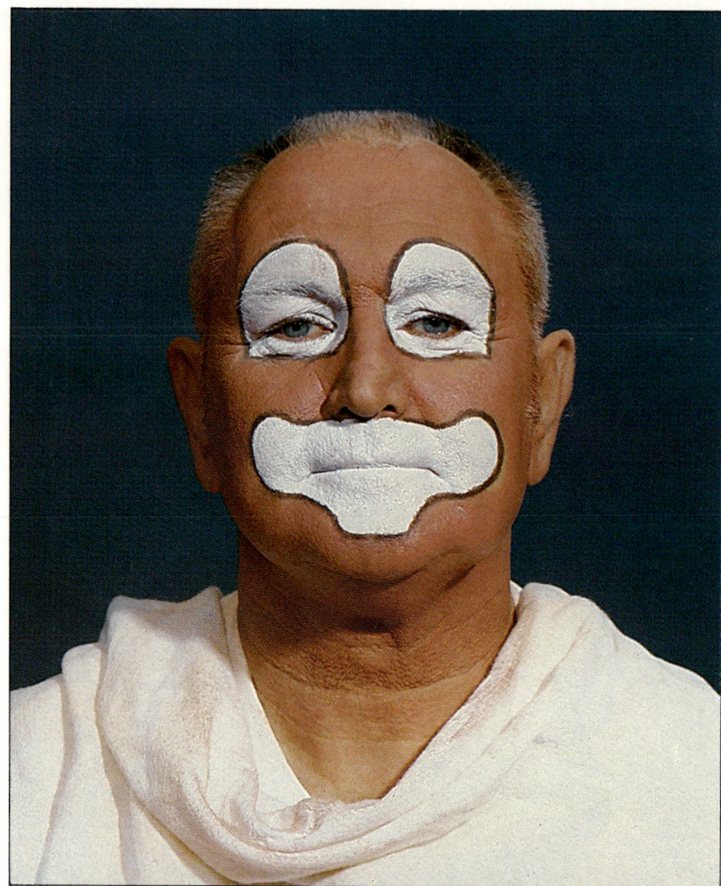

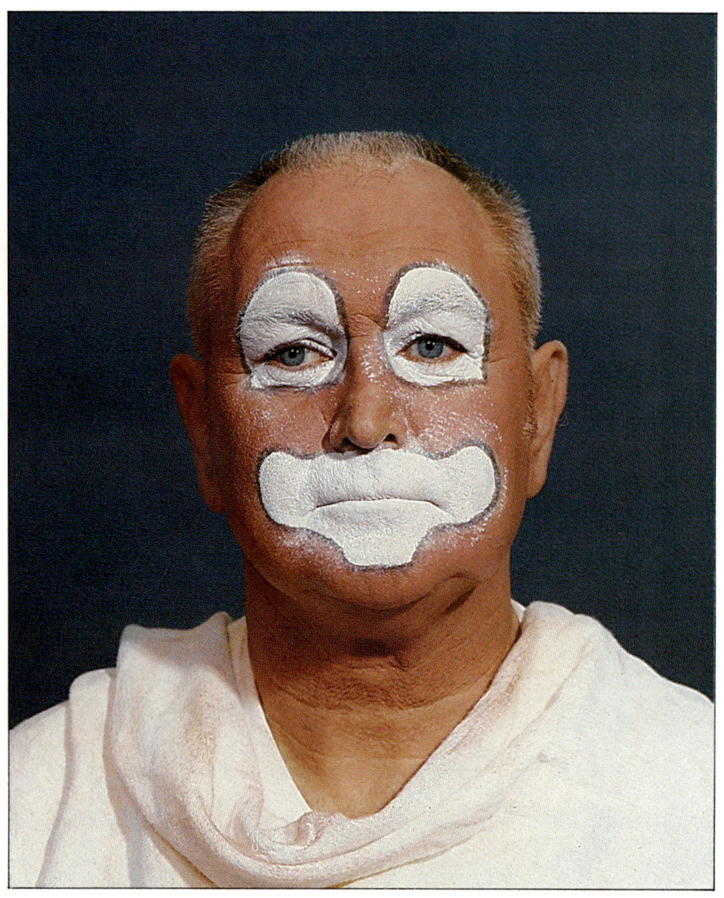

7

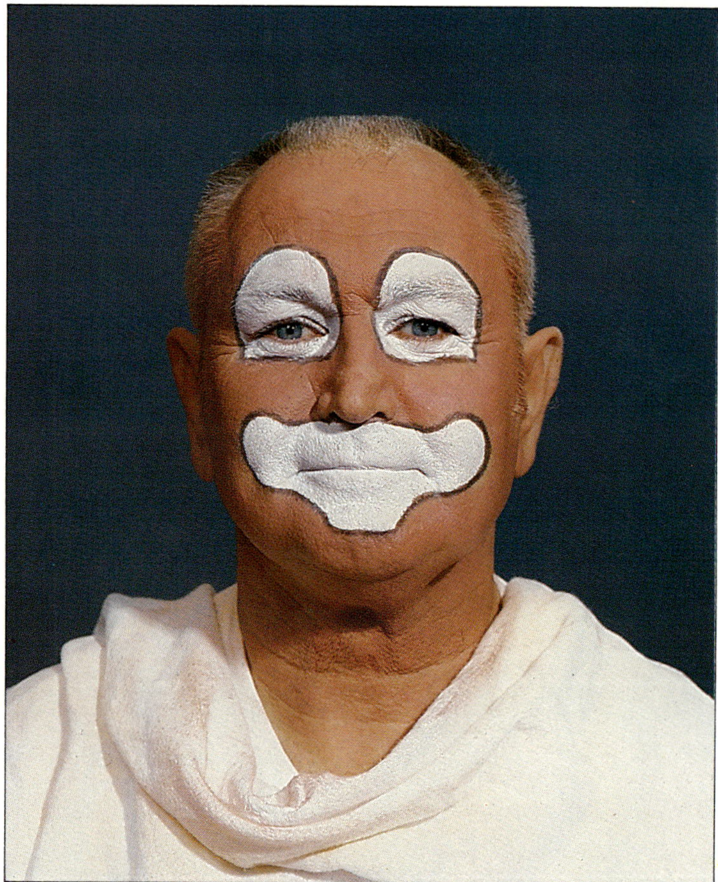

8

9

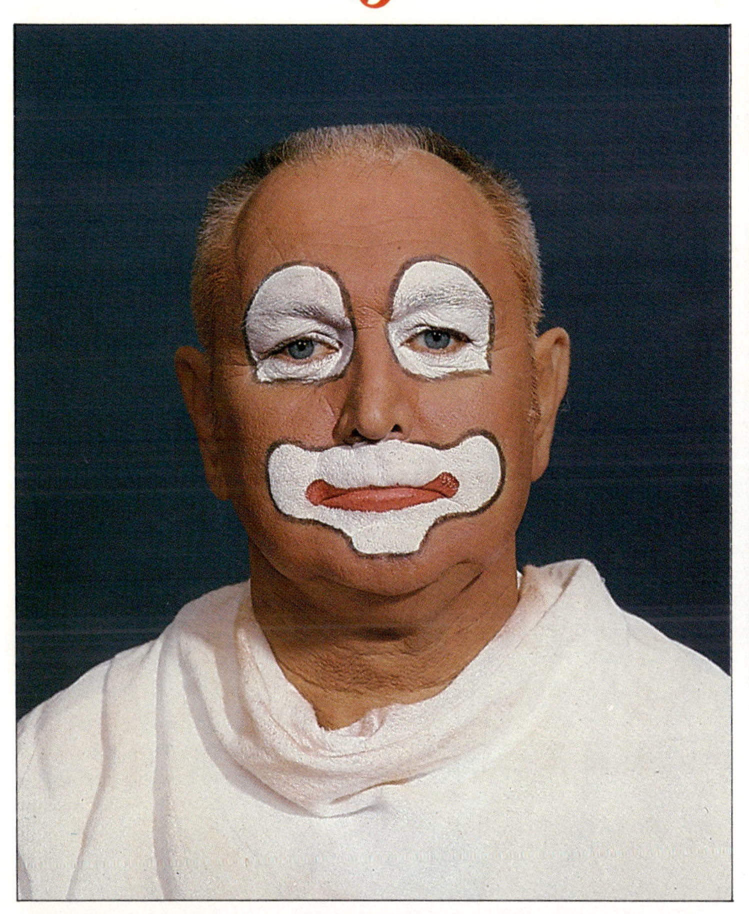

10

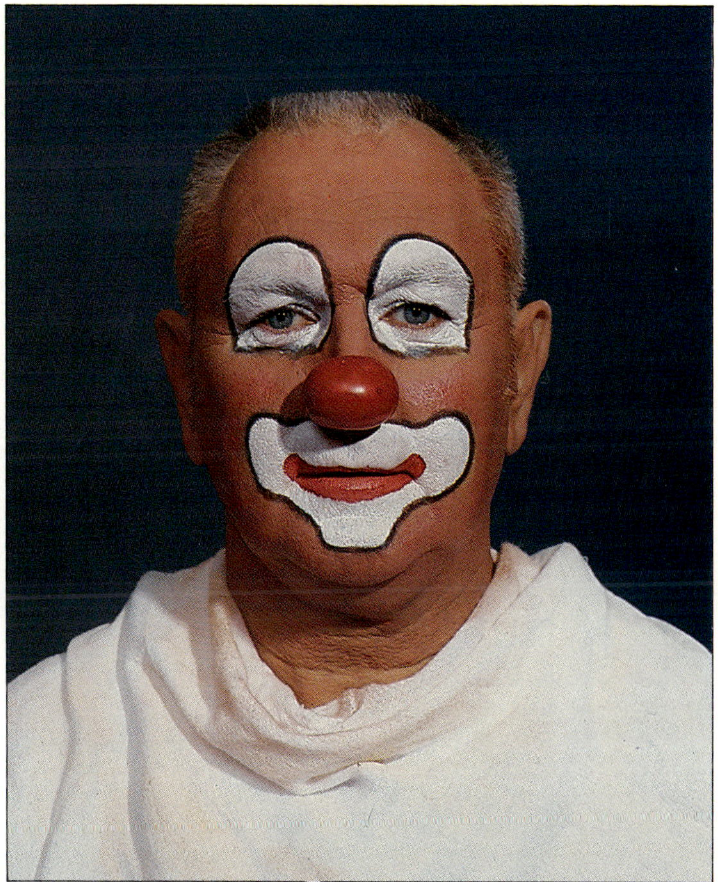

11

12

13

14

4 Makeup

Makeup is the most important single element of clowning. The face expresses the style of clown and his emotion. Through the face we see character and, symbolically, life. The dominating white reminds us of death, and the bright colors or lines remind us of life. Exaggerated features let us know we are to see life expanded and enlarged.

The makeup is also the mask of the clown. The person puts his mask on and is transformed from everyday life to the life of the clown. Each time the mask is put on, the person moves into the world of the clown, brush stroke by brush stroke.

The process of putting on the face is a ritual for the clown. It is the moment he escapes from a world of pain and fear into the fantasy of the clown. In the world of fantasy perfection reigns—at least, perfection from the clown's viewpoint. Through this world of fantasy the clown can present the truth of Christian life: the beauty of Christ, the grace of a loving Heavenly Father.

There are four major styles of makeup to be dealt with in this discussion: white face (neat), white face (grotesque), auguste, and tramp. The technical process of applying makeup is not difficult. The clown will need makeup materials and preferably a lighted mirror.

The beginning clown should learn to apply his own makeup. In the long run this is more practical. If a clown troupe depends on two or three people to apply everyone's makeup, valuable time is lost. The troupe is limited by the fact that these people must be present. Some beginners will have difficulty at first, but diligence and experience will more than compensate for any lack of "artistic skill."

Most clowns will eventually build their personal makeup kit. (See page 35.) However, many church groups should also supply communal makeup. Particularly is this true with a youth clowning troupe. A communal supply can ensure that makeup is always available and can also provide a good variety of colors and application materials.

Makeup generally falls into two categories: grease paint and Pan-Cake (water soluble). Both have advantages and disadvantages. Grease paint is the traditional and oldest type of makeup. It provides bright, strong colors. However, grease paint can be irritating to the skin, and some people are simply allergic to it. Also, it can be messy to apply and requires baby oil, cold cream, or an astringent to remove. Pan-Cake is easier to apply and is washed off with soap and water. However, Pan-Cake is not as bright as grease paint. In outdoor performances on a bright day, Pan-Cake can look faded, especially when compared to grease paint. Pan-Cake does work well indoors in most cases.

In recent years there have been several technological breakthroughs in makeup. The most recent is a new type of grease paint that is water soluble. As this makeup becomes more readily available, it will be ideal for church clown troupes. Soap and water are all that are needed to remove the makeup. When purchasing makeup, check with the major companies on the availability of this type of makeup.

This discussion will deal primarily with grease paint. However, at the end of the description of grease paint application for the four types of clowns, you will find techniques for applying Pan-Cake.

White Face Clown

The traditional white face clown has white over the entire face with red and black features. He may be "neat" with a normal size mouth, nose, and eyebrows, or he may be grotesque with outlandish features and a gigantic nose. Usually the white face clown wears a skullcap to cover his hair. He also may wear a wig. Skullcaps can be purchased at most costume, magic, or theatrical supply houses. A skullcap can also be made from a white nylon stocking. Pull the stocking over the head and mark the place for the ears. Also measure where it should be gathered and cut off. Remove it and make the appropriate cuts.

This is the process for applying white face makeup:

1. Apply a base of cold cream or baby oil. Rub evenly all over the face, neck, and ears. Pat off the excess with a paper towel. Men should be cleanly shaven before this process begins.

2. Apply "clown white" by spreading with the fingertips. Rub it in well, over the entire face, eyelids, neck, and ears (if ears will show).

3. Pat or slap lightly over the entire white area with the fingertips. This will give the makeup a smooth appearance.

4. Powder with a white powder and powder puffs, or use a white sock containing baby powder. Pat the powder on all white areas. You cannot use too much powder.

5. Remove the excess powder with a soft bristle makeup brush or a shaving brush. Brush lightly until all excess powder is removed. Set by spraying a fine water mist, or gently pat with a damp sponge.

6. Apply colored features to the face. Beginners may wish to lightly sketch the size of the mouth, eyebrows, and other features before using the colors. Sketch lightly, with a brown pencil, the shape of the features. Apply a diluted red on the mouth area. Use a lipstick brush to shape the mouth. Experiment with different shapes and sizes. Some suggest that red be applied to lower lip only and then extend up from the corner of the mouth. However, some people have small mouths, making it necessary to cover the upper lip also. You may wish to remove the white in the area the color is to be applied before applying the color. Use a Q-tip or tissue paper. Be careful not to smear. A makeup brush can be added to apply the color. This will ensure sharp edges. Set with a fine mist spray or a damp sponge.

7. Powder the colored areas very carefully with a second powder sock. Be careful to touch only the red and not get out into the white.

8. Carefully brush off the excess, using the same procedure as in step 4. If the red color is diminished too much by the white powder, wet your fingertips with water and gently pat over the colored area, restoring the brightness.

9. Add black outlines with a black grease stick, grease pencil, or outline pencil. Outline around the mouth, add crow's feet at the corners of the eyes, and draw on eyebrows or other character lines. The black lines do not need to be set with powder. Remember to keep the face simple, using few character lines. The more markings used, the more broken up the face becomes. Too many markings may also be confusing.

10. Add skullcap, wigs, hats, or other accessories.

Auguste Clown

The auguste clown, often termed a "character clown," has the same exaggerated features as the grotesque white face. The basic difference is that the auguste uses flesh color as the dominant color. White is used around the eyes and red mouth.

The auguste requires two main base colors, plus a red mouth. Be careful that you use the proper powder sock and shaving brush for each color. You should never use the sock or brush for white on any other color. You may use the other powder sock and brush on both the flesh and red, simply by turning it to a different spot. Or you can use a small sponge powder puff on the red lips by dipping it in baby powder.

This is the process for applying auguste makeup:

1. Apply a base of cold cream or baby oil to the face, neck, and ears. (See Figure 1.) Pat off the excess with a paper towel or tissue.

2. Outline the boundaries of the mouth and eyes (where the white goes) with a grease pencil. (See Figure 2.) This will give you the areas to color. Remember, two base colors are used. Beginners may wish to mark the areas first with a light brown pencil.

3. Apply the base color (flesh) which will take up the largest area of the face. (See Figure 3.) It is not necessary to be exact on the boundaries at this time. Pat or slap with the fingertips the colored flesh area to even the application of the color. Be sure to apply flesh to the neck and ears also. Set with a fine mist spray or damp sponge.

4. Powder down the flesh color. (See Figure 4.) This will seal it and cut the glossy appearance. Use a powder that matches the flesh color if possible. Apply the powder with a powder sock or a powder puff.

5. Brush away all excess powder, using a shaving brush or soft-bristle powder brush. (See Figure 5.) All excess powder must be removed so that it will not interfere with the application of makeup on the rest of the face.

6. Apply the second basic color (white) in the same manner the flesh was applied. (See Figure 6.) Be careful that it does not run or smear into the flesh base. Use a lipstick brush or small makeup brush to shape the areas and bring the colors right up to each other.

7. Using the second powder sock, again powder down (see Figure 7), and brush off the excess, using a second shaving brush or makeup brush. (See Figure 8.)

8. Apply the mouth, using a diluted red. (See Figure 9.) See makeup instructions on how to dilute. Apply the red with a lipstick brush or makeup brush.

9. Powder down the red area and brush off the excess. Be careful not to smear other colors.

10. After all character lines and color features are applied and set, add a rubber nose (see Figure 10), wig, hat (see Figure 11), or other accessories. (See Figure 12.)

Tramp Clown

The tramp clown is traditionally a sad, sorrowful, vague character. He has a white mouth, with white around the eyes, and a black beard. Flesh color covers the rest of the exposed face and neck.

This is the process for applying tramp makeup:

1. Apply a base of cold cream or baby oil. Smooth evenly over the neck, face, and ears. Remove the excess by patting with a paper towel or tissue.

2. Outline the features with a grease pencil. This will help you know where to apply the different colors. Beginners may wish to experiment with size and shape of features. Use a light brown pencil to do this.

3. Begin with the lightest makeup first—in this case it is the white area around the mouth. If you make a mistake or slip a little, the dark beard will correct it. Apply the white makeup to the area of the eyes. This gives the tramp character a bleary-eyed look and a surprised expression.

4. Apply the flesh-colored base to the neck, face, and ears.

5. Up to this time no powder has been used. This is done for a purpose. This permits the beard to be feathered into the flesh and white colors. Feathering can only be done while the colors are still wet and glossy.

6. Apply black to the beard area, bringing the edge of the beard into the wet flesh color. Do the same for the white area around the mouth. This takes much practice and gives the appearance of a real beard and not the harsh lines as seen on other types of clown faces. Set with a fine mist spray or damp sponge.

7. Powder down the entire face and remove the excess lightly. This will set the makeup.

8. Add character lines around the eyes and on the forehead if needed.

9. The natural hair of the clown is used in the tramp character. Rumple the hair as desired.

10. Add a hat (sloppy or neat) and other accessories.

The makeup processes described above are the major steps in makeup application. Clowns will discover their own shortcuts and special techniques with experience. The intent is to bring to life the painted mask of the clown. The person should do whatever is necessary to achieve that result.

Makeup Kit

All major theatrical makeup companies market clown makeup. Churches will save money by buying makeup in large containers. Small containers may be inexpensive, but they won't last long. Large containers of clown white are especially important.

A large fishing tackle box will make a good container for a communal makeup kit. Clowns may wish to use small fishing tackle boxes for personal makeup. Again, clowns are encouraged to purchase their own makeup and maintain their own kit. Some churches will, however, find it cheaper and more efficient to maintain a central makeup supply for the clown troupe.

The following list includes materials necessary for greasepaint application:

1. Clown White (buy it by the can).
2. Red greasepaint (check shade with company before ordering).

3. Flesh-colored greasepaint.
4. Blue, green, or other special colors.
5. Red grease pencil.
6. Blue grease pencil.
7. Black grease pencil.
8. Baby oil, cleansing cream, and/or astringent.
9. Makeup mirror(s).
10. Baby powder or makeup powder (white and flesh colors).
11. White cotton socks (for powder socks).
12. Shaving brushes, inexpensive 1-inch paint brushes, or soft-bristle makeup (powder) brushes.
13. Lipstick brushes and makeup brushes.
14. Q-Tips.
15. Paper towels and other tissue paper as needed.

Optional Supplies

1. Lighted makeup mirror.
2. Cosmetic cape, or towels to put around shoulders during makeup application.
3. Cloth or plastic hair bandeaux (to hold hair back from forehead).
4. Eyebrow pencils.
5. Small pencil sharpener.
6. Sponge powder puff or other powder puffs.
7. Small soft brush (to scratch nose).
8. Spirit gum to hold nose in place.

Clown white, greasepaint, and grease pencils will need to be purchased at makeup, costume, or theatrical supply houses. Occasionally drugstores in small, rural communities will carry these items. Any drugstore or makeup house can order greasepaint. Other materials can be purchased in local drugstores and discount houses.

Clown white, greasepaint, and similar items that are purchased in bulk can be shared by all clowns. Divide the makeup from the large containers. Place it in small plastic pill bottles. These can be obtained at local drugstores and are inexpensive. Or use 4 × 4-inch plastic squares. Give each clown squares with the necessary makeup for one application.

Pan-Cake Makeup

The basic steps in applying Pan-Cake are similar to those of greasepaint. However, powdering is usually not necessary, and soap and water are used to remove the makeup. Follow these steps in applying Pan-Cake.

1. Cleanse the face with soap and water.
2. Apply clown white or flesh-colored Pan-Cake with damp sponge. Mark with a light pencil the areas for other colors, and leave these blank.
3. Apply red to the mouth and other areas as desirable. Apply other colors at the same time. Apply with a sponge or makeup brush. A brush will be necessary to make sharp lines and edges of colors.
4. Outline and accent with a liner brush, using a black water-base Pan-Cake.
5. Add skullcap, wig, hat, or other accessories.

Pan-Cake Makeup Kit

The Pan-Cake makeup kit includes the following items:

1. Clown white.
2. Black.
3. Red, flesh, blue, and other colors as necessary.
4. Sponges.
5. Brushes.
6. Pencils (brown and black).
7. Mirror(s).
8. Plastic containers for water.

Pan-Cake makeup is available from costume, makeup, magic, and theatrical supply houses. (See Bibliography.)

Makeup Hints

1. To make a powder bag, use a clean cotton sock. Fill the toe with baby powder and tie the sock off about an inch above the toe. The powder bag should be about the size of a lemon. If tube socks are used, more than one bag can be made from each. Simply tie both ends of the second bag. Two powder bags are necessary because one should be used on white areas only. The other should be used on flesh and red areas only. The sock used for red and flesh will need to be emptied of powder and washed every few times it's used. Some clowns use a small sponge rubber powder puff for the red mouth area. Just dip the powder when you're ready to powder. Use lots of powder.

2. A man's shaving brush works well to brush away excess powder. At least two are necessary: one for the white and one for the colors. Be careful to always use the proper brush on the right color.

3. A lipstick brush (that retracts) works well when applying one color next to another color. This is easy to handle and gives a very clean definite line. Some clowns achieve the same result with their fingers. The brushes must be kept clean. To accom-

plish this, place a small amount of baby oil or cleansing cream in the palm of the hand. Carefully work the bristles back and forth in the palm of the hand. Continue the process until all color is out of the brush and wipe it clean.

4. To dilute red greasepaint, add a few drops of baby oil. Take some red greasepaint and place it in a jar. Add the baby oil and mix well. The diluted mixture is easier to apply than when it is straight from the tube.

5. To remove makeup rub baby oil, cleansing cream, or astringent over all made-up areas of the face and neck. Wipe the makeup off with paper towels. Repeat the process until all traces of the makeup are gone. Wash with soap and water.

6. To apply a rubber clown nose, use spirit gum and/or a small rubber band to hold it in place. If spirit gum is used, the face area should be free of greasepaint where the nose will be applied. Elastic thread, purchased at a sewing center, can be used to make a rubber band for the nose. Attach it to both sides of the rubber nose and run it around the back of the head. If you are going to be very active, the elastic band is generally more secure and should be used.

7. If your nose itches after you have your face on, use a small soft brush to scratch with.

8. Men, remember to always shave before applying makeup.

9. Bearded clowns who do not wish to be tramp clowns can make up the part of the face that is exposed, usually as a white face, with accents on the nose and eyes.

10. Black and dark-skinned people can be white face clowns also.

11. To clean shaving brushes and makeup brushes, wash with warm soapy water and rinse well. Press out the excess moisture and set aside to dry. If the brush you use on the flesh and red areas is really dirty, you may need to use baby oil. Place some in the palm of your hand and work the bristles back and forth in it, as suggested previously for the lipstick brush. After removing most of the color, wash it in warm soapy water. Rinse well, press out the moisture, and set aside to dry.

Beginning clowns should experiment with their makeup until they are completely satisfied. The clown must be completely satisfied with his face to be free to communicate to the audience.

Additional information on makeup is available through books listed in the Bibliography. Many makeup companies will also supply free clown makeup descriptions on request.

Note: Major portions of the makeup chapter were taken directly from *Clowning Is . . .* by Ernie and Jean Liebig, © 1980. Used by permission.

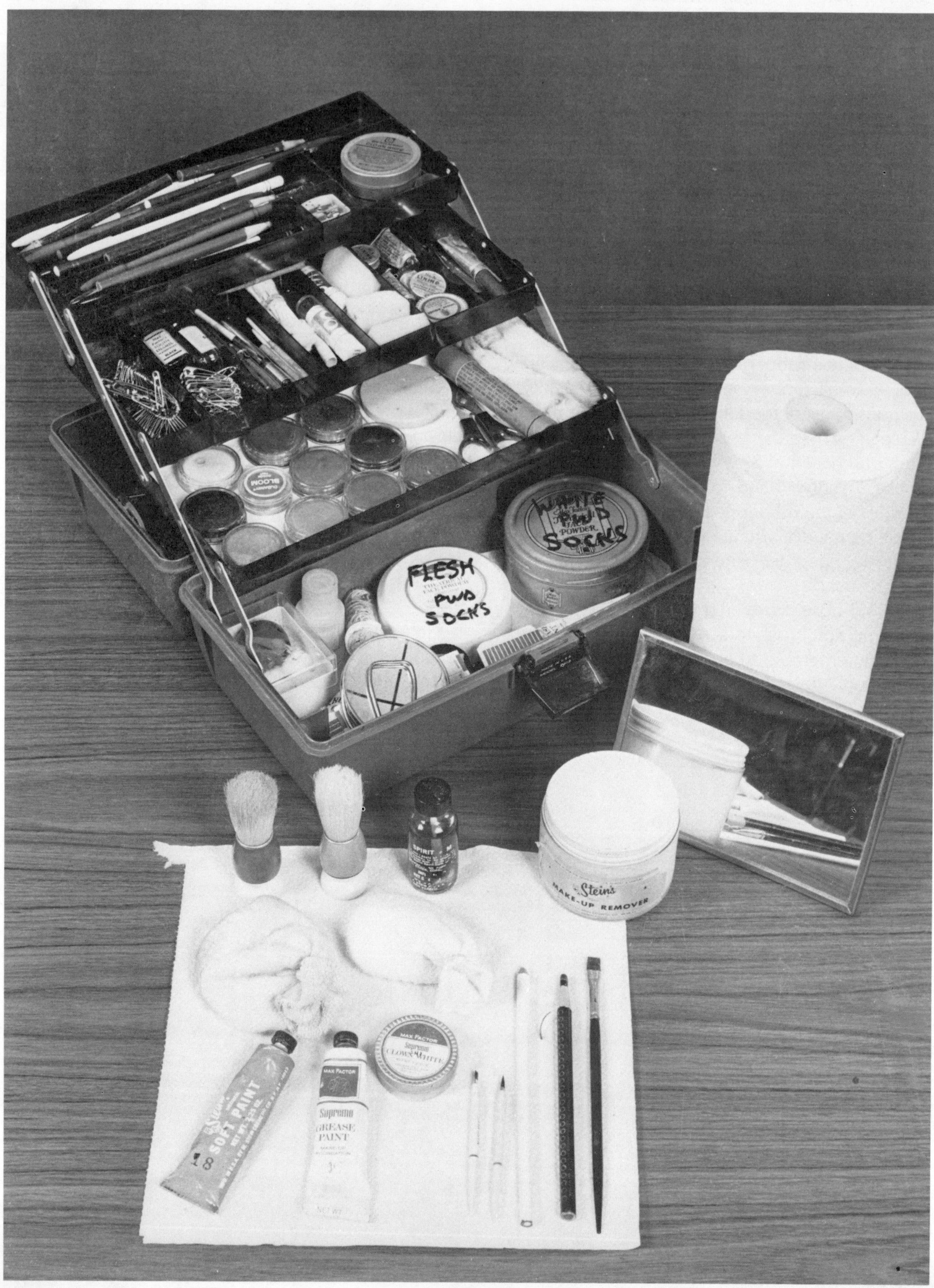

WHITE
PWD
POWDER
SOCKS
FLESH
PWD
SOCKS
BLOOM
Stein's
MAKE-UP REMOVER
SOFT PAINT
MAX FACTOR
Supreme
GREASE
PAINT
MAX FACTOR
Supreme
CLOWN WHITE

A Christian Clown Troupe, after a hard day of ministry!

5 Costume

The term *costume* is the word an audience uses in viewing a clown. From the clown's point of view the costume simply consists of his clothes. The clothes worn by a clown are generally referred to as his wardrobe.

Clothes express the clown's character. In chapter 1 the clown is described as being larger than life, an exaggeration of life experiences that are basic to all people. The costume is another statement of that characteristic.

Generally, clowns are dressed in outlandish clothing. Basic elements of the clothes become exaggerated expressions of normal human attire. Buttons may be enormous and brightly colored. Ties of the bow tie or straight tie variety are often very large. Suspenders, belts, buckles, shoes, hats, and other items tend to be oversize.

Clown clothes are often ill fitting and appear to be ridiculous to the average eye. However, a closer look and evaluation of a professional clown's clothes reveals many subtle comments. How ties are worn, how shoes are laced, how hats are worn—all become strong statements about the character.

The audience is quick to notice when something looks wrong. A white face, neat clown makeup just doesn't go with a shabby, tramplike costume. When the audience learns more about the character through the actions portrayed, the match looks even worse. The poor choice of clothing can destroy everything the character is trying to achieve.

Take time when shopping for clothes for your clown character. Fit the clothes in style, line, color, and feel to the character and makeup. The wrong bow tie can ruin an otherwise perfect suit. Once the basic suit is selected, take the same pains with accessories.

Clowns must also be practical when selecting a wardrobe. A bright wool coat may look good in a store, but it will be unbearably hot on a midsummer day. Enormous clown shoes may look wonderful, but try walking several miles in a parade, or climbing stairs.

Select clothes that can be easily cleaned. Wash and wear are the best. Clothes that must be dry-cleaned should be reserved for very special occasions. Otherwise the cost for regular cleaning can be prohibitive.

Clothes should be selected based on the type of activities the clown will be involved in. For example, if your character is going to ride a bike or unicycle, balloon pants will continually be in the way. Children like to pull and tug at clowns. At least one outfit should be selected for primarily working with children. Jugglers need to be able to move the arm freely. Simply consider the character and major types of activities when selecting the wardrobe.

Another major consideration is weather. On a hot summer day, wear minimal clothing under the suit. Obviously the fabric must be thick enough so the audience cannot see through it. Lightweight clown clothes are usually OK in the winter because thermal underwear and other clothes can be worn underneath.

Some clothes will be necessary for rainy, muddy weather. A mission Vacation Bible School may be held in a very dusty area. The clown may be required to sit or even roll on the ground. A wash and wear outfit will be a necessity in this environment. A raincoat may ruin the appearance of the character. Avoid rain when possible, but if one must perform in a light drizzle, wear clothes that are appropriate.

Most clowns prefer to purchase and maintain their own clothes. However, some church clown troupes may find it advantageous to store and maintain costumes used in the ministry. These may be purchased, constructed, or collected over a period of time. Clowns who drop out of the troupe may be able to donate some of their costumes or accessories to the group.

A special drive to obtain donated clothes for clowns can turn up exciting and interesting items, all free. Even donated clothes that are not usable can often be cannibalized for their buttons, pockets, collars, lining, or other parts that can be used in clown suits.

Stored costumes should be under lock and key. Otherwise many people will borrow a clown suit for "little Johnny's birthday" and never return it. Or if they do, it may be torn, dirty, or defaced in some way. Nothing will destroy the spirit of a clown quicker than finding his favorite suit ruined.

An alternative to the above problem is to provide some costumes, usually old, for members of the church to borrow. For example, a children's choir director may want to wear a clown outfit for choir promotion day. A costume just for the purpose of being loaned can be a real plus for the overall ministry of the church. Many professional clowns shudder at the thought of amateurs running around in a clown suit with no makeup. However, the Christian clown troupe's first concern is ministry. Professionalism is important, but second to ministry.

Developing the Wardrobe

The actual process of finding clothes for the clown begins by rummaging through one's own closets. Old shirts, coats, dresses, blouses, hats, etc., that have not been worn for years may be just right. They may even come close to fitting.

Next, hit every Goodwill store or other used clothing outlet in your area. Look for madras tuxedo jackets, swallowtail coats, and any bright suit that might be useful. A reasonably plain basic coat can be decorated with many accessories that will make it perfect for the character. Often men's slacks in wild plaids or prints are available in used clothing stores. A cutoff pair of men's slacks may be perfect for a lady clown.

Another suggestion is to find a two-piece white twill uniform often worn by chefs or bus boys. These can be trimmed with braid or buttons to suit your taste. They wash well and make a neat-looking costume.

Remember to also shop for accessories. Look for top hats, ties, bow ties, buttons, pins, shoes, socks, suspenders, glasses, wigs, and other similar items. Keep in mind the idea of cannibalizing one outfit and adding those parts to another. Lining, pockets, and collars from one suit coat may go well on another.

Constructing a Costume

One-piece clown suits worn by white face and some auguste clowns normally need to be constructed. (See Figures 13, 14.) Major dress pattern companies offer patterns for one-piece clown suits. A two-piece pajama pattern can also be adapted.

For most men, these patterns need to be enlarged. Clowns are very active, and additional space for movement should be available in the stride. If the pattern calls for six or seven yards, you will be safe to buy nine yards and another yard and a half for the collar.

The white face and auguste clowns should have an accent at the neck, possibly ruffles or a tie. Either a bow tie or an exaggerated long tie works well. Make these separate from the suit so that they can be easily removed for cleaning. Vel-Cro is readily available in fabric stores and is ideal for attaching the ruffles and ties to the suit. Vel-Cro is also useful for other accessories to be used on the suit. Make at least two collars for each suit, using contrasting colors. This gives the suit a different look and helps to provide more flexibility in your suit.

The best fabrics for clown suits are: 50 percent polyester broadcloth, cotton twill, satins, and other fabrics with 50 percent polyester. Satins are beautiful, but difficult to care for. The fabric should be wash and wear if possible. Avoid 100 percent cottons. They are easily wrinkled.

Accessories are an important part of the suit. Generally avoid sequins because they cannot be washed. Some possible accessories are: ruffles, ties, bows, pompoms, pointed collars, bells, large buttons, badges, name patches, hearts, felt-figured pieces, lace, rickrack, seam binding (wide and narrow width), fringe, ribbons, and flowers. Many other items may also be useful for special characters. Patches may also be used. Auguste clowns might use a dark coat with a bright lining. The coat is then torn in places so that the lining shows through.

Most clowns wear gloves, primarily to cover the skin. White face clowns normally wear white gloves.

Auguste clowns may wear special colors or white. The gloves need to be thin so the clown can move the fingers efficiently. Work gloves look bulky and are difficult to move in. Band gloves or puppet gloves work well. These are available in most communities. Air Force dress gloves are another possibility. These are well constructed and cover the wrists well. They are available at most Army-Navy Surplus stores. If you are doing balloon sculpture while wearing gloves, cut the fingers out of the glove to facilitate your work.

When cleaning clown suits, check first the neck ruffles or collars, the wrist, and gloves. These seem to get dirtier than other parts of the suit. A good cleaning treatment with an effective liquid detergent to these spots before a regular washing will usually remove all traces of makeup. Regular washing without treatment will not remove the stains and sometimes even sets the stains, making it almost impossible to ever remove them.

Clown wigs are readily available for purchase in costume, makeup, magic, and theatrical supply houses. (See page 44.) They can also be purchased at some special interest stores. Occasionally they are available in major discount chains.

Another possibility is to purchase a wig kit. These kits, including wig base and hair along with instructions, are available from some wig manufacturers. Theatrical supply houses often have regular theatrical wig kits available. Bright-colored hair may work well for a clown wig.

Wild-colored fake fur can be cut in thin strips and sewn to a band. The band can be part of a hat or used independently. Cut the pieces the desired length of the wig. Yarn and dyed mop string is another possibility. However, constructed wigs must fit the makeup, costume, and character. The wig must also look good. A sloppily constructed, misfitting wig may do more damage than good to the appearance of the clown.

The right hat can often make a wig or skullcap look good. Almost any style of hat has been used by some clown at some time. Top hats, bowlers, and straw hats are favorites. Miniversions of hats are also popular. The white face clown often will have a skullcap topped by a miniversion of one of the hats just mentioned. Hats must be secured by a rubber elastic band. Sewing elastic is available at sewing centers and variety stores. Fit the band to reach down behind the head, not under the chin. A minihat may have to be secured under the chin. Avoid running the elastic band under the chin if possible. This will call attention to the strap, and may be uncomfortable for the clown.

Oversize clown shoes are very expensive and not very practical. (See page 44.) They look great in a picture, but are difficult to move around in. Leather shoes can be painted with bright-colored enamel or fluorescent paint. Canvas shoes can be dyed with either regular cloth dye or liquid acrylic paint. (See page 44.) Acrylic paint is easier to use because it can be used undiluted, straight from the jar. These shoes will be easier to move in and more comfortable.

Some clowns may need to wear glasses. Clown glasses are available from clown supply houses. Prescription lenses can then be fitted to the glasses. Or paint and decorate an old pair of your own glasses. The glasses will drastically affect the makeup. Have the glasses handy when applying makeup so they can be slipped on and off. Plastic, nonbreakable lenses should be used. An elastic band will also be needed to hold the glasses on. The same type of band used on hats and noses can be used.

Several pairs of bright-colored, large suspenders are a necessity for any wardrobe. Look for very broad striped suspenders. Try to find suspenders with leather loops on the ends to fit over buttons on the pants. These are more secure than thin metal clips. These clips can break or slip loose during a performance. The clown must then use one hand to hold up his pants while he tries to gracefully complete a performance. An alternative is to get some strips of leather, remove the metal clips, and sew the strips into the suspenders.

An exception is suspenders worn by skiers, campers, and backpackers. These usually have strong metal clips. These suspenders are available in skiing shops. They can usually be found in stores that specialize in camping, backpacking, and outdoor sports.

Above all, be practical when selecting a clown wardrobe. One hint is to sew large pockets into two- and three-piece suits. Clowns need to carry candy, balloons, and often personal valuables. These need to be concealed, but easy to get to. Large hidden pockets are a necessity. In constructed one-piece suits sew in special pockets that appear hidden. These may have zippers on them that are on the side of the costume and invisible unless seen at a very close range.

The clown's wardrobe can be just as practical and exciting as a personal wardrobe. Each year will bring new clothes and see old ones thrown away or given away. The clown's wardrobe consists of the clothes of his or her character. Everyone wants clothes suitable for the occasion—even clowns.

Note: Major portions of this chapter are taken from *Clowning Is . . .* by Ernie and Jean Liebig, © 1980. Used by permission.

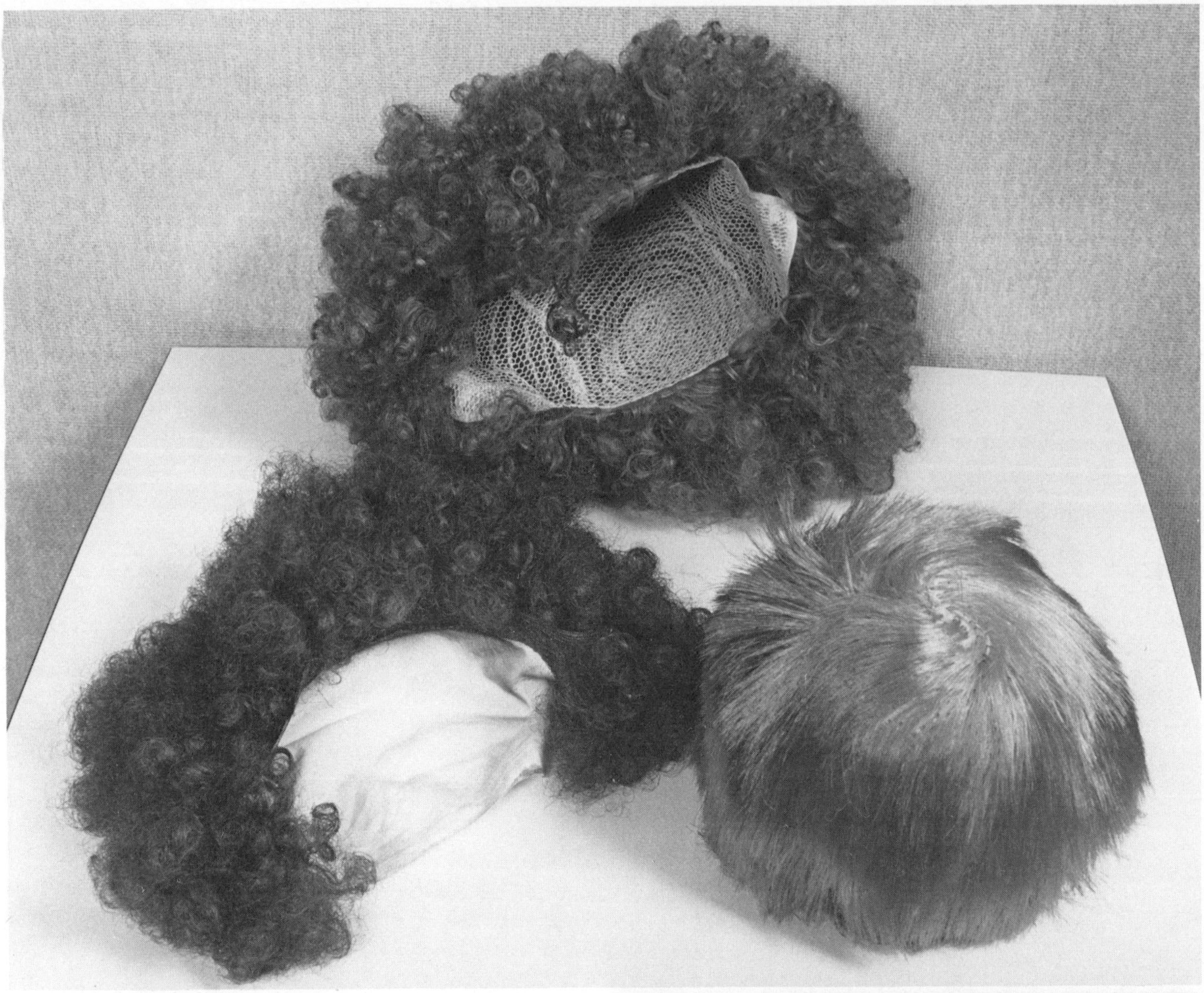

6 Props

Props are the tools of the clown. They are aids for the clown to use in the process of communicating the gospel. Some props are large, others small; but each has a specific purpose. The clown handles each prop with the same expertise and pride with which he applies makeup and selects a wardrobe.

Props have several specific jobs. They may be a physical means of drawing attention to the clown or what the clown is doing. They may strictly be used to entertain and induce laughter from an audience. They may be a physical means of communicating love between the clown and his audience (candy, kisses, "Love" balloons, etc.). Or they may be used to illustrate the truth the clown is projecting. The last is particularly important when expressing Bible truths, actual Scripture, modern parallels to scriptural parables, and similar ideas.

Some props require special skills. Juggling, riding a unicycle, and performing magic are examples. Other props are sight gags. Oversize cameras, binoculars (see page 53), and golf clubs are examples.

For the purposes of this book, props will be divided into the following categories: skill props, pocket props, oversize props, costume props, animals and puppets, balloon sculpture, musical instruments, and magic.

Skill Props

Juggling is a basic clowning skill that is very useful. (See page 55.) Three-item juggling is not difficult to learn and can be very entertaining for an audience. Items most often juggled include: balls, apples, oranges, bowling pins, plates, and rings. Once the clown learns basic juggling technique, almost any item can be juggled. To juggle three balls, follow this procedure:

1. Stand facing a blank wall with the arms to the side. Bend the arms at the elbow with palms facing up. Movement will be with the palms and wrists only moving up and down. Avoid side movements.
2. Practice tossing the balls one at a time from the right hand to the left, and vice versa. They should be tossed in an arc that reaches nose height. Practice to make each toss exactly the same height.
3. Now take two balls in the right hand and one in the left hand.
4. Toss one ball from the right hand into the air.
5. When the first ball reaches the top of the arc, toss the ball in the left hand.
6. Catch the first ball with the left hand.
7. When the ball tossed by the left hand reaches the top of the arc, toss the other ball in the right hand.
8. Catch the second ball tossed with the right hand.
9. Continue juggling by alternating tosses between hands. Remember to toss a ball each time a ball reaches the height of the arc.
10. Now practice, practice, and practice.

Beginners will learn quicker by spending a lot of time at step 2. Tossing the balls accurately is the key to success. Another good exercise is to juggle two balls with one hand. To accomplish this hold both balls in the right hand. Toss one ball up and slightly toward you. When it reaches the height of its arc, toss the second ball the same way. Catch the first ball and toss it when the first ball reaches the height of its arc.

Work to be as smooth as possible. Juggling is very rhythmical. Once you learn to toss the balls accurately with both hands and you get the rhythm, the rest is easy.

Initially, be sure to juggle three items of equal shape and weight.

Riding a unicycle is another skill that can look spectacular but is not difficult to learn. Athletes and experienced bike riders will probably learn quicker than others. To learn to ride a unicycle, follow these steps:

1. Adjust the seat height so you can sit on it with your toes touching the ground.
2. Sit on the unicycle by a wall or rail and on a flat surface. Hold the rail or wall with one hand while you get your balance. Initially you may want someone to stand on the other side to steady you.
3. Use a forward and backward rotation of the wheel with your feet to maintain balance.
4. Lean the body slightly forward.
5. Pedal forward in a steady, smooth motion, using the upper torso to maintain balance.
6. Spread arms to each side for additional balance.
7. To stop, put both feet on the ground and catch the seat of the unicycle in one hand. Use the other hand for balance.

Some people find it easier to start by staying stationary and simply moving the wheel forward and backward about six inches until they can control their balance.

Bicycles can be adapted for use in parades and similar clowning situations. One adaptation is to put a small wheel in front and a large wheel in the rear. Another is to take a 26-inch bike with the front and rear wheel spokes off-center. A third idea is the two-story bicycle. It is about twice as high as a normal bike. Raise the handlebars, seat, and sprocket about three feet. With practice you may even be able to do wheelies on this bike.

Walking on stilts is yet another skill that can be learned fairly easily. Start with short stilts. Place the foot rests about twelve to eighteen inches off the ground. Practice walking. Gradually increase the height of the foot rests.

Pocket Props

Pocket props include almost anything that can be carried in the pockets of the clown suit. (See page 54.) These may include sound instruments, simple magic tricks, and similar items. Candy and other handouts would be considered pocket props.

The following is a list of some simple pocket props:

1. Telephone. This actually is the receiver with a cord. A battery-operated ring is carried in the pocket. Push a button, the phone rings, and you answer. (See page 54.)
2. Magician's wand that collapses.
3. Flower that wilts.
4. Fan that falls apart.
5. Rubber band tricks.
6. String tricks.
7. Shoelace tricks.
8. Handkerchief tricks. (See page 54.)
9. Rope tricks. (See page 51.)
10. Sponge balls.
11. Colorful bandanas.
12. Large feathers.
13. Church fan.
14. Feather duster. (See page 55.)
15. Canvas "tote" bag to carry things in.

Oversize Props

Oversize props are everyday items that are enlarged to an enormous size. Here are a few. Many of these you can construct yourself.

1. Binoculars. (See page 53.)
2. Light bulbs.
3. Roller skates.
4. Golf bag and clubs.
5. Pencil or pen.
6. Cup.
7. Plate with knife, fork, and spoon.
8. Pocket watch that runs.
9. Book of Knowledge.
10. Alarm clock.

Costume Props

These are takeoffs on the clown's costume. They are usually extremely large or odd shaped. Generally they are used with gags involving audience members. (See page 52.)
Some examples are:

1. Glasses.
2. Wigs.
3. Hats.
4. Ties.
5. Baggy pants.
6. Noses.
7. Suspenders.
8. Bells.
9. Masks.
10. Capes.

Animals and Puppets

Stuffed animals and puppets can be used in many different ways. (See page 50.) A clown may walk around with a large teddy bear. Another clown may have a small puppet that he uses for talking to himself or others. Many stuffed animals can be adapted for puppets by removing some of the stuffing and making a slit in the bottom or back for the clown to place his hand.

Puppets may have their own stage. One or more clowns stand in front of the stage and talk to one or more puppets behind the stage. Puppets may even be dressed as clowns.

Muppets or hand puppets (with moving mouths) are best if they are to appear behind a stage. The moving mouth adds life to the character and makes it easier to understand what is being said. Some type of amplification will be necessary. Small amplifiers with the speaker, amplifier, and one or two inputs in one small box are now available. These are ideal for use with clowns.

The following basic techniques are important in handling muppets.

1. Syncronize the movement of the mouth of the puppet with the voice of the puppeteer. As a general rule open the mouth of the puppet on vowels or syllables.
2. Keep the puppet's head level so the eyes of the puppet are looking at the eyes of the audience.
3. Enter and exit by moving the puppet up and down in small movements as if the character is walking.
4. Generally puppets are childlike and speak in short, clipped sentences.
5. Add life to the puppet by whistling, humming, or making other human sounds. The definition of a puppet is any inanimate object that takes on human characteristics.

A puppet stage can be anything that provides a barrier between the puppeteer(s) and the audience. A refrigerator crate that has been painted or covered with colorful fabric will work fine. Cut an opening about forty-five inches from the bottom for the puppet to appear. A curtain may be hung over the opening. The puppet will enter under the curtain and appear in the opening.

Another possibility is to make a small frame from one-inch plastic pipe. Hang curtains on the plastic pipe to mask the puppeteer.

(For additional information on puppets consult *Using Puppetry in the Church,* Broadman Press.)

Balloon Sculpture

Balloons and clowns naturally go together. In recent years special balloons have been manufactured that permit sculpturing animals and other objects. Two of the most common balloons used for this purpose are "pencil" and "apple" balloons.

Pencil balloons come in various sizes and thicknesses. The most common number for sculpturing is #260. The number means that the balloon is approximately two inches wide and sixty inches long. A letter following the number will refer to the thickness of the wall of the balloon.

To make an apple from an apple balloon follow this process (see page 56):

1. Inflate the balloon, leaving a couple of inches at the end not fully inflated. Tie off the end.
2. Using the forefinger of one hand, press the end not fully inflated through the center of the balloon until you can reach it with the other hand.
3. Holding the end of the balloon with the other hand, gently twist the tied off end around the other end (which is inside the balloon). Two or three twists should hold it in place.

To make a dog from a pencil balloon, follow this process (see page 56):

1. Inflate the balloon, leaving several inches at the end not fully inflated. Tie off the end.
2. Twist three places from the tied-off end about two inches apart. (To twist, take the balloon in both hands and rotate one hand one way, the other in the opposite direction. One gentle twist will hold the balloon in place.)
3. Connect the first twist and the third twist. Twist these two connections together. The head and ears are formed.
4. Twist three more places down the balloon about three or four inches apart.
5. Connect the first twist and the third twist in this grouping. Twist these two connections together. This forms the neck and front legs.
6. Move down the balloon about six inches and make three more twists about three inches apart.
7. Connect the first and third twist of this grouping. Twist these together. This forms the body and back legs. Leftover balloon will be the tail.
8. Features can be painted on the dog with a felt pen.

Musical Instruments

Numerous musical instruments and sound makers can add to the clown's performance repertoire.

Here is a list of some instruments you may want to use:

1. Kazoos. (See page 53.)
2. Harmonica.
3. Jew's harp.
4. Ukelele.
5. Guitar.
6. Battery-operated electronic guitar. This is a new instrument available in toy stores. It is programmed to play several tunes.
7. Tambourines.
8. Recorders.
9. Accordian.
10. Autoharp.

Kazoos are fun if the entire troupe sets up a choir. One clown can conduct while everyone plays. Another fun activity is a bottle band. Fill bottles to various levels with water. Incorporate the water tub base and similar instruments also.

Magic

Clown magic is composed primarily of small hand tricks. These are aimed at inducing laughter from the audience or illustrating a point that the clown is making. People interested in full magic shows don't need clown makeup and suits.

Local magic shops have plenty of tricks suitable for the clown. Also, order catalogs from major suppliers. Select appropriate tricks.

Clown troupes can carry these tricks in special boxes. The boxes may be labeled "Brain Box" or another name. Here are some selected tricks clowns may wish to use:

1. Locking scissors.
2. Disappearing cane.
3. Breakaway fans.
4. Rope tricks (including knot tricks) (see page 51).
5. Multiplying balls.
6. Mouth coils—streamers.
7. Interlocking rings.
8. Sympathetic silks.
9. Bending umbrella (see page 52).
10. Flash paper (ignites when it hits water).

Suitcase gags are often corny, but almost always enjoyed by an audience. A briefcase may have a sign on the side of it entitled, "First Dog in Space." When the clown opens it up there's a hot dog hanging from a piece of wire. Another briefcase may be entitled "Chicken with 3 Feet." When it's opened there's a rubber chicken with three one-foot rulers.

Book gags can also be fun. (See page 53.) A special sight gag may be constructed and painted to look like a book. For example: One might be titled, "What I Know About Women." It's actually composed of two pieces of plywood. When it's opened there's nothing inside.

For additional information on props and how they're used, consult the chapter on Performances.

Happy
THE CLOWN

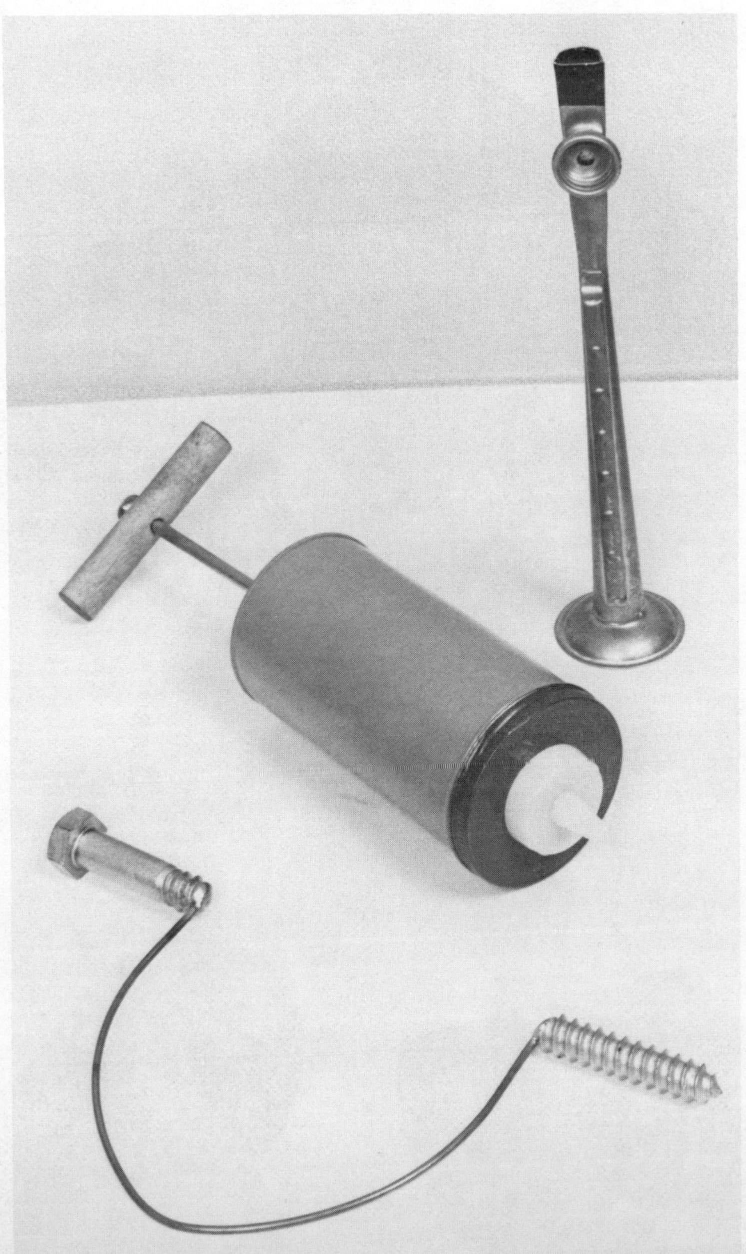

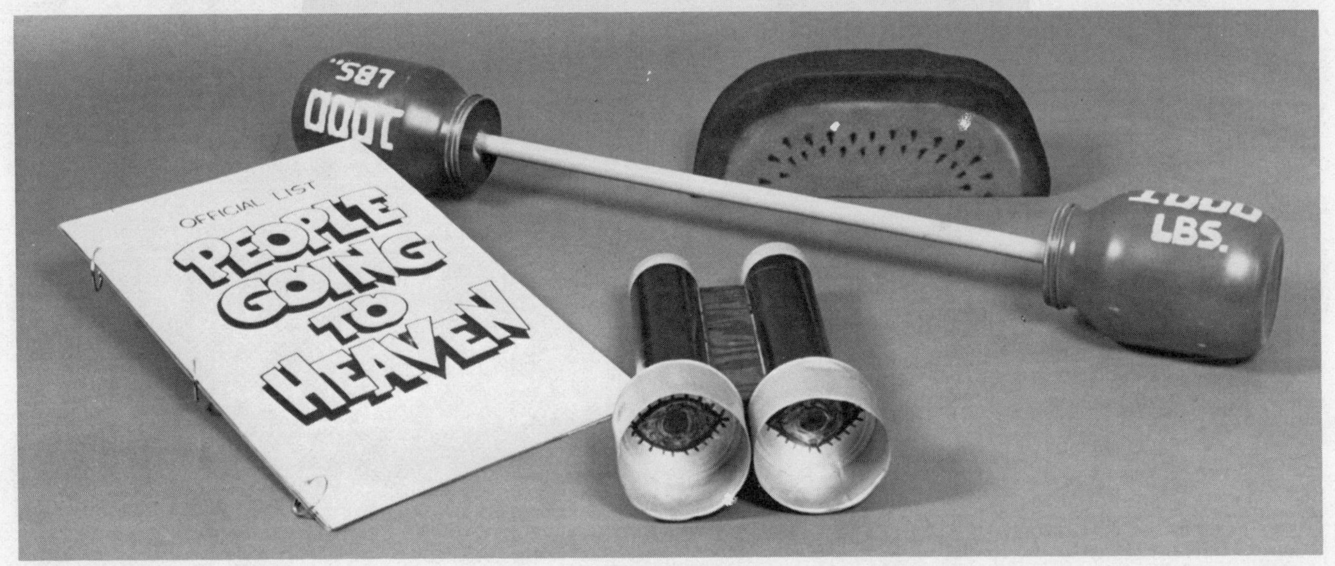
LBS.
1000
OFFICIAL LIST
PEOPLE GOING TO HEAVEN
LBS.

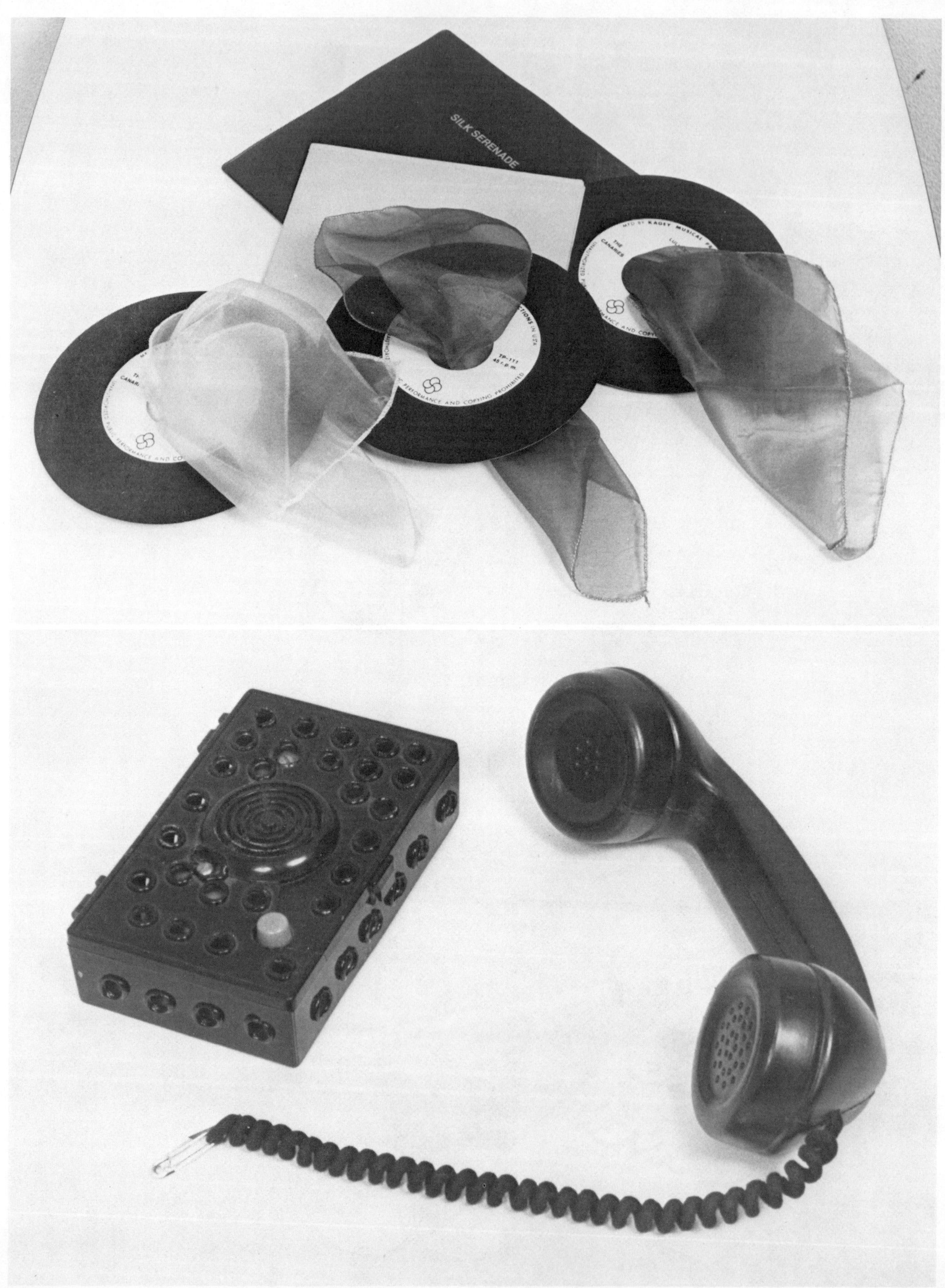
SILK SERENADE

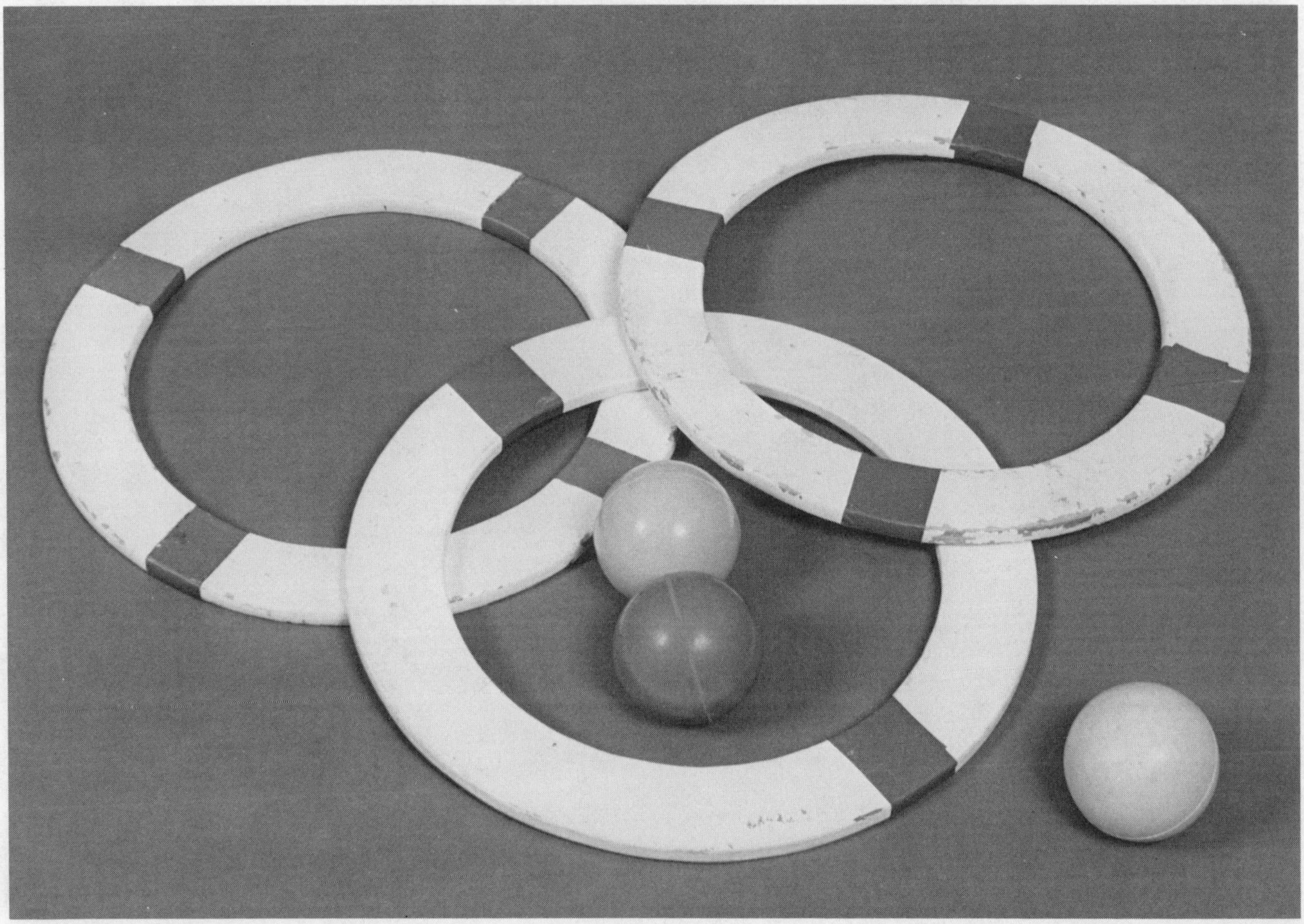

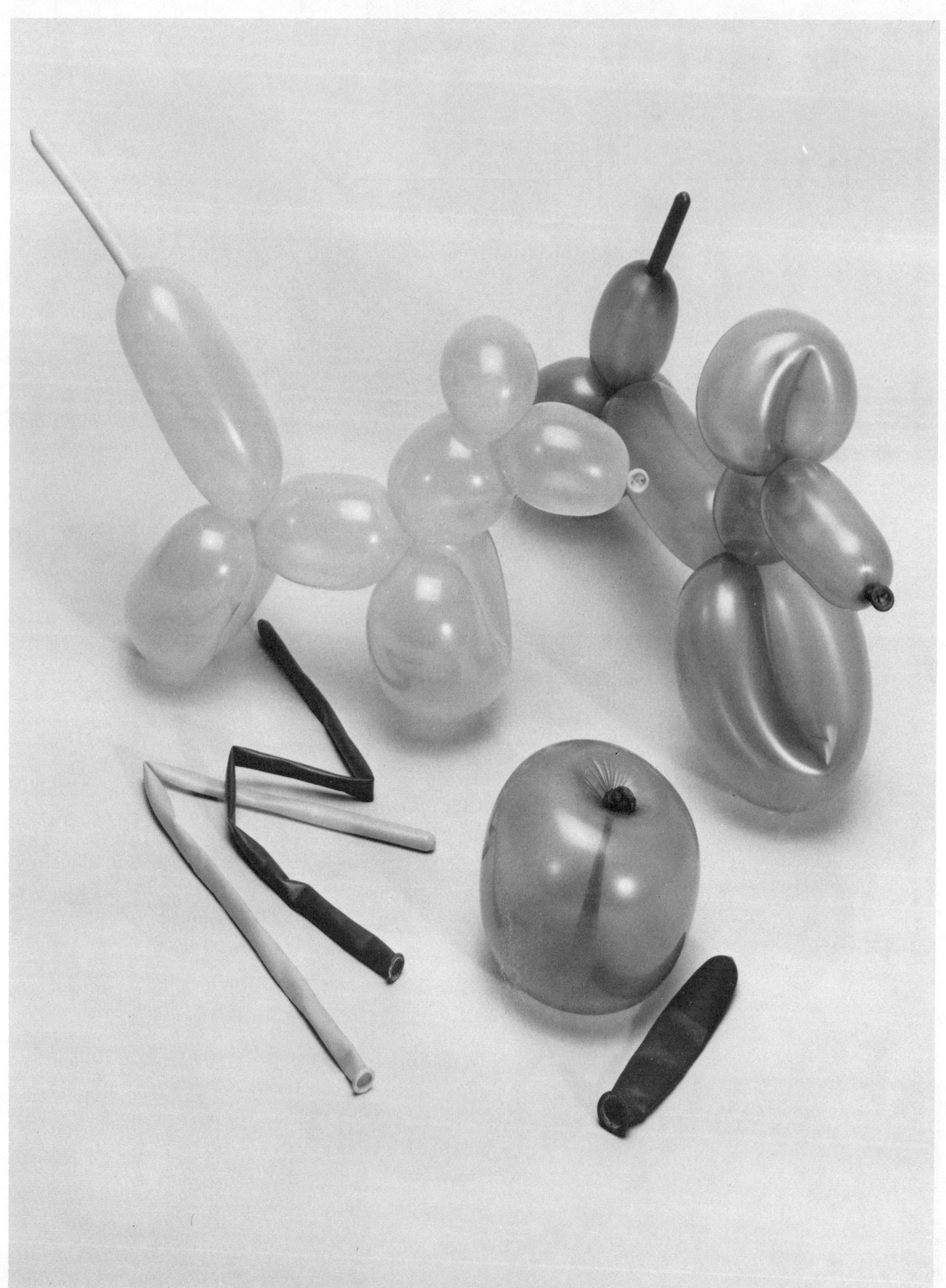

7 In the Spotlight

Performance Techniques

Performing is what clowning is all about. All the practice. All the special skills. All the time spent developing character, makeup, costume, and the handling of props is aimed at one thing—performing. Performance technique really cannot be taught; it is basic and instinctive in all people. The more clowns perform, the better performers they will become.

The first step in performing is to plan the activity well in advance. Prepare all performance routines until they are almost perfect. Obtain as much information as possible about the audience, the length of the performance, and the place the performance is scheduled.

Scout the location in advance if possible. Check the performance area and have it cleared of any objects that will be in your way. If a trip exceeds twenty to twenty-five miles, it may be necessary to apply makeup and dress at the site. Make sure adequate space and facilities are available to do this.

At least one person not in clown attire should accompany the group. This person will drive the car or van. They will keep the group together and handle logistical problems. For example, on a parade they will need to let the group out at the start of the parade and pick them up at the end. It can be very exhausting to walk a long parade and then walk back to a parked vehicle. This person can also handle unruly children during performances. It's difficult for the performer to handle an unruly audience member without being rude. The uncostumed person can also carry valuables, handle special props, take care of the travel makeup kit, and similar chores.

Use some type of travel cases for all props, makeup, and other special equipment. The cases can be old suitcases that are brightly painted, or they can be specially constructed. They need to be lightweight and durable. Larger props will require specially constructed cases.

Rehearse setting up for a performance and striking after a performance. Everyone in the troupe should be assigned duties that will make the setup and strike very professional looking. In some places the audience may already be present when you arrive. The way the troupe sets up equipment can gain or lose the respect of the audience.

Do not plan too many activities in one performance or too many performances in one trip. Select a few things that you can do well and omit the others. Long clown performances are rarely successful. Thirty minutes is just about the maximum length for one performance. Performances that must exceed this length should be broken up with intermissions, musical entertainment, or something else. The length problem is compounded when one clown is performing alone.

Always have an alternate plan if something doesn't work. What will you do if the performance must be cut short for some reason? What can be easily omitted? What will you do if you need more activities to fill the time? What if the music doesn't work? A million things can go wrong in a performance. Prepare in advance for as many of them as possible.

Let's say a performance for a children's home has been scheduled outdoors. When you arrive it begins to rain. Much of your program was planned with lots of space outside to execute routines, tricks, jokes, etc. Suddenly you find yourself crammed in a small room with seventy-five children. What will you do?

What if you are in a parade and it begins to rain? What are the alternatives? One solution is a colorful umbrella that will match or contrast with your wardrobe. If the umbrella is not available, you might want to remove your hat and wig and let your hair go straight down. Greasepaint will hold up fairly well in a light rain.

Always carry a small makeup kit. Several performances in a row on a hot summer day may require periodical touchups of the makeup. You want to look your best all the time if possible.

Ensemble Playing

A clown troupe must work together as a team. In most cases this is easier said than done. Ensemble work requires total familiarity and confidence in what the other members of the troupe are going to do.

Many routines are based on bold, slapstick, physical actions. These require complete concentration and teamwork to be successful. The action has a specific rhythm, and it is important that every participant in that action move in the same rhythm.

Timing is crucial. Certainly it is important to "pick up cues" in routines. However, it's also important to know precisely when another clown has completed his act. The next performer should begin instantly after the previous performer is finished. Dead spots or pauses can destroy an otherwise delightful presentation.

Work to think together and move together as a troupe. Try to instinctively mold yourself into the group. With experience, a troupe working for these goals can become a beautiful unit to watch.

Age Group Considerations

Performing for Children

Children love clowns, provided they are old enough to understand and accept the characters. Generally, children under four are not old enough, so avoid performing for the young preschoolers.

The first rule in clowning for children is to get to the level of the child. If the clown encounters a child one on one, stoop, squat, or kneel to the child's level. When performing for a group, build the material around subjects of interest to children. This is the way you get to their level. Once you establish a line of communication with the child, it is easier to teach important information.

For example, use illustrations that involve characters or some element of the characters that children are familiar with: Sesame Street characters, the Muppets, Donald Duck, Mickey Mouse, and others. You may have to prepare the children in order to use Jesus as a character they can understand. Many children today have never been to church and never had a Bible. They have never heard of Jesus. You must be careful that they do not identify Jesus with Mickey Mouse, Donald Duck, etc.

Use the imagination of the child. Their imaginations are very alive and vivid. Capitalize on this in performance settings. Use ideas such as, "Let's imagine this is a beautiful forest with beautiful flowers, beautiful birds, beautiful trees—everything is bright and beautiful." This would be an excellent lead-in to a flower illustration.

Protect the performance area from the children. Otherwise they will want to examine props, touch you, look behind the puppet curtain, and on and on. One way to do this is to use a specially constructed low rail you can place between yourself and the children. Another way is to bring a brightly colored rope which encircles the performance area. Children are warned that if they cross the rail or rope they will not be asked to help in the performance.

Keep performances short. It is better to do two or three fifteen-minute sets than one forty-five-minute performance. Use as much variety as possible in the performance. Mix music with tricks and routines. Follow a loud routine with a soft activity. Follow a small activity with a large and boisterous one. The more variety used in the performance, the better the chances of sustaining audience interest.

Leave props in cases until you are ready to use them. Then remove them for the performance and replace them as soon as you are finished. Children will pick up favorite items and carry them home. They will even reach in your pockets for props. Store pocket tricks in inside, hidden pockets if possible.

Use as much audience participation as possible. Ask the children questions. Pick one child at a time to help you with some of the activities. Give children the opportunity to become totally involved in your presentation.

Performances for Adults

Adults do not escape into the world of their imagination as quickly as children. However, a well-thought-out performance can eventually lead them to escape into the world of fantasy and the clown.

Begin performances with themes and ideas that directly relate to them. Build on emotions they are very familiar with—love, hate, fear, etc.

Remember that usually clowns do the opposite of what would be normal action. Build on this concept. Use routines such as the "Weight Lifting" scene. Involve audience members in the performance. Use tricks and jokes that will catch them off guard.

Adapt the size of the action to the size of the crowd. The larger the audience, the more exaggerated the action should be.

Incorporate background music with selected activities. This gives a professional feel to the performance. Use live instruments and group singing as appropriate.

Performances for Senior Adults

Follow the same guidelines for senior adults as with adults. However, the physical movement can affect some activities.

For example, in nursing homes, you will need to circulate from room to room. Be conscious of sound and use soft instruments and quiet props.

Personal contact is very important. Speak to each person. Ask them what they know about clowns. Be sure to tell them why you are clowning.

Touch is very important to these people. Touch them; let them touch you. Use puppets and stuffed animals. Let them touch the puppets and animals. Talk to them through the puppet.

Leave them something if possible. A balloon sculptured animal would be perfect. Or leave them a regular balloon with "Love" on it or a similar phrase. Remember why you are there and the "love" you are communicating.

Scenes to Promote Special Programs and Activities

1. A clown enters a worship service or Sunday School department with an eight-foot-long Styrofoam baseball bat. "Strike Out King" is written on the bat. Someone asks the clown what he's doing and he says, "Going to strike out." He is then asked, "Why are you going to do that?" The clown replies, "Because it's time for the church softball league to start." A person asks, "Well, don't we need some hits, too?" The clown replies, "We won't unless some of the rest of you clowns get out there and take your time at bat." Then he exits.

2. Enter the room or sanctuary with a straw broom and move down the aisle, sweeping the floor. The dialogue can go something like this.

"Hey, what are you doing, clown? Can't you see we're having church here?"

"Yes, yes I can!"

"Well, what are you doing?"

"Well, I'm sweeping!"

"What do you mean you're sweeping? Are you the janitor?"

"No, I'm not the janitor."

"Well, what are you doing?"

Clown points broom at audience and says,

"We want to make a clean sweep and find all those members on your Sunday School rolls. Let's get busy and have a clean sweep for the Lord!" (Exit.)

3. Three clowns of different sizes enter, holding the blank side of a sign to the audience. They stand in front of the audience and pause. Finally the smallest clown turns his sign to the audience. It says, "WE." The second clown turns his sign and it says, "WANT." The largest clown then turns his sign and it says, "YOU." Then all three clowns point at the audience and say "in Church Training" or whatever is being promoted.

Scenes for Use in Worship

These are selected scenes to show some of the ways clowns can be successfully used in worship experiences. In every case it is important that the congregation be familiar with a basic theological concept of the clown. The worship experience can be completely destroyed if the congregation views the clown as a slapstick circus figure.

"The Rose." A clown enters with music playing and pantomimes that he wants the congregation to sing. He takes a hymn book and they follow suit. With his fingers he counts the page number for "Share His Love," or a similar hymn. Then he leads the congregation in singing the hymn. The clown may also pantomime during the singing. At the conclusion "The Rose" begins to play. (Atlantic Records—sung by Bette Midler.) The clown pulls a rose from his sleeve. He reaches toward the audience as if giving the rose to them.

"God Gave the Song." The character enters without costume and makeup and briefly describes the similarities in the clown and the Christian life. The process of applying makeup is the process of discovering new life. When the makeup and costume are complete, the character is a new creature. Soft music plays in the background. The clown moves to a table in front of the audience and quickly applies makeup and steps into costume. (Note: Pan-Cake is quicker to apply and may work best in this scene.) He concludes by pantomiming with "God Gave the Song" from *Alleluia.* Then the congregation sings the chorus "Alleluia!" The clown exits during the singing.

"Inner Self." The clown enters in costume and makeup and acts out a passage of Scripture or relates a biblical truth. Then the character begins to remove his makeup and costume in front of the audience. At the conclusion he states that our outer actions must be consistent with the inner spirit. If we project the love of Christ in our inner spirit, we must also do it through our outer actions.

Other possibilities for incorporating clowns in worship are to promote various programs in the church. The clowns may enter with a sign and walk across the podium and say nothing. Or they may act out a short skit promoting the project or activity.

Some clown troupes will want to report back to the church about experiences in retirement homes, hospitals, malls, etc. The troupe can enter in full costume and makeup. They can share with the audience their experiences through pantomime, action and words, or special scenes.

- Here's a scene designed to go with Matthew 5: 38-44.

A man and woman clown enter. They are wearing dark glasses. They sit down on a bench, similar to a park bench, each on an end of the bench. The man is reading his Bible. He notices that the woman is cold. He looks in the Bible, then stands and begins taking off his shirt. She stands and places her glasses on the bench. He hands her his shirt and she slips it on. They sit down. When they do, he sits on her glasses. She is very angry. She jumps up and begins hitting him. He checks in the Bible and then turns the other shoulder. She grabs a stick and begins hitting him with it. He checks in the Bible. Then he gives her his glasses. He takes the stick, breaks off the end and hands it back to her in the shape of a cross. They exit.

The minister immediately reads Matthew 5:38-44.

- Many different scenes can stem from a "Gift Box."

1. One or more clowns enter the church with a large box marked "Gift Box." They place the box on a table at the front of the church and take out offering plates. The offertory is played and the offering collected.

2. One or more clowns enter the church with the "Gift Box." They open the box and take out a nativity scene as a Christmas carol is sung.

Background music can add strength and mood to a scene presented in church. Music is particularly valuable for silent clowns. Easy-listening music works very well in the background. The secular music of Percy Faith and Endre Castilantis is good. Johnny Mathis' "Feelings" is a good number. So is Sammy Davis, Jr.'s "Going to Build a Mountain." Another good one is Debby Boone's "You Light Up My Life." Danny Gaither's "Sometimes Hallelujah" is also good. Many contemporary gospel recordings also work well. Other good recordings are the Percy Faith arrangement of "Amazing Grace"; "Share His Love"; and Diana Ross' "Reach Out and Touch Somebody's Hand." There are hundreds of songs similar to these that will work well.

- The following information is a description of a creative communion service led by Holice Turnbow in costume and makeup. He has used this successfully at retreats, camps, and other settings.

The audience must be introduced to the clown and the purpose of the clown before the service can begin. Holice sometimes does this verbally without costume and makeup. Then he applies makeup and costume so that they can see the transformation. He concludes this by leading a hymn.

To start the service the clown enters with a large denim shopping bag. The bag has a number of props, including a handful of balloons with "Love" printed on them. The clown warms up the group by passing out the balloons, gesturing that he loves them, etc. In the background contemporary music is playing. The music deals with love. The clown may hand a balloon to someone and ask him to blow up another one and hand it to someone else. Another way to do this is for the clown to enter with a large garbage bag that's already filled with the balloons. Another possibility is to bring a bag of unmarked balloons that are already blown up. Take a felt-tipped marker and let someone write something on a balloon and pass it to another person. Other props such as chocolate candy kisses and red hearts can be handed out to achieve the same effect.

After four or five minutes of this warmup the clown makes a big bow and backs up. He stumbles over a large apple basket and a smoke bomb goes off. This gets the clown's attention, and he notices that the basket is filled with assorted things: several yards of aluminum foil, a huge loaf of bread, a gallon jug of grape juice, paper cups, two sticks—one shorter than the other—a big red piece of yarn, a piece of round Styrofoam, a little vase with a flower in it, and a very colorful piece of cloth.

The clown sets up a table which becomes the communion table. He holds the sticks up in the shape of a cross. Then he hands the sticks and the red yarn to someone in the audience and they tie it in place. After everything is set on the table, the clown notices the aluminum foil and wonders what to do with it. He decides it must be to cover the cross, bread, and juice. So he wraps each item with the foil.

At this point two or more people enter to assist. They may walk in as robots with white faces and no markings.

They walk up to the clown near the communion table. The clown offers them communion; but because it's wrapped up they can't get to it, so nothing happens. The clown realizes something is wrong and removes the foil. As he removes the foil, they come out of their robot state. The clown begins to share the bread with them and with the audience. The two robots take the cups and juice and begin to serve everyone present. When they return to the front, the clown serves them and everyone takes communion together. The services ends with the singing of "Blessed Be the Tie" or another appropriate song.

Improvising Scripts for Clowning

Many of the best scenes clown troupes use are original. Some will be discovered by accident. However, literally hundreds can be developed by spending a few minutes during each rehearsal to explore new ideas.

Select special phrases, everyday human situations, or main topics of interest. Pinpoint characters and possible outcome. Then ad-lib the script. Nothing should be written down. All of the action and/or dialogue stems from the clowns.

Discuss the scene that has been ad-libbed. Make any changes and alterations. Then run the scene again. After running through a scene four or five times you can refine it for performance.

Many corny ideas can be hysterical when performed by clowns. The secret is how the clowns execute the dialogue and action.

One of the best resources for ideas is the newspaper. Look for unique stories, advertisements, headlines, pictures, etc. Then think about an approach to the idea that is opposite of what is obvious. Select characters and try it out. The comics page is another place to get ideas for scenes.

Remember, scenes should be very short. In some cases two or three lines may do the trick. In others fifteen or twenty will be required. Keep scenes under five to six minutes in length.

Serious pantomimes for worship can be developed in the same way. Visualize a passage of Scripture, a hymn, or an anthem. Then take the image and bring it to life with clowns.

The same process can be used for developing special promotional scripts and special occasions. For example, suppose the clown troupe is to perform for a choir banquet. Possible scripts might be based on:

1. "Let's Turn Over in our Hymn Books"
2. "Sam Jones Sings Flat"
3. "Susie Smith Sings Sharp"
4. Pantomime the choir director (exaggerated gestures)
5. "Hand out pieces of music" (clown tears up a sheet of music and hands out the pieces).

Look for phrases that are humorous if taken literally. Exaggerated action can also bring to life an otherwise dull scene. Here are some possible scripts for a sports banquet:

1. "Get on the Ball": A coach yells at a player practicing basketball. The player gets on top of the ball and it deflates.
2. "Foul": Referee with whistle blows whistle and yells "Foul." A clown enters with a dead chicken.
3. "Strike Three"
4. "Batter Up"
5. "Clipping"

The possibilities are endless. Pick words and phrases that your audience is familiar with. Then give them a different meaning, and humor will be the result.

Comic Clown Scenes

Here are several selected comic scenes that will work well in fellowships or other performances.

"People Who Are Going to Heaven": The clown has a large fake book with the above title on it. The clown then takes a list of names of people in the audience and looks for their name in the book. On some he smiles and gives a big nod. On others he looks sorrowful and shakes his head no. To end the routine, walk up to the pastor and slowly shake the head no.

"Golf Anyone?": A golfer and his caddy enter with an enormous golf bag and club. They begin to argue over who can hit the ball the greatest distance. The argument builds until the golfer angrily takes the ball out of the bag. Then he reaches his hand back for the club and yells, "Let me have it." The caddy, who is still angry, hits the golfer, who falls down. The caddy runs offstage.

"Weightlifting": Two large cans are attached at the ends of a broomstick or round pole. The piece is brightly painted and has 500,000 LBS. written on it. One clown announces a contest to see who can lift the weight. Three other clowns volunteer to try. They try to figure out a way to lift the barbells. While they are arguing about it, a small clown dressed like a janitor enters behind them, picks up the barbells with one hand, and drags them offstage.

"A Higher Court": A clown enters with a ladder, looking very sad. Another clown asks him what's wrong. He says he lost his court case. The other clown asks what he's going to do now. He yells angrily, "I'm going to take the matter to a higher court," and thrusts ladder in the air.

Resources

Magazines and Newsletters

Calliope Magazine. Published by Clowns of America, Inc., P. O. Box 3906, Baltimore, MD 21222.

Clown Chatter Magazine. 12100 S. 80th Ave., Box 323, Palos Park, IL 60464.

Church Drama Newsletter. Published by Church Recreation Department, Baptist Sunday School Board, Nashville, TN 37234.

Church Recreation Magazine. Published by the Church Recreation Department, Baptist Sunday School Board, Nashville, TN 37234.

Shoddy Pad. Published by the Office of Communications Education, United Methodist Communications, 1525 McGavock, St., Nashville, TN 37203.

Source Monthly, "Newsletter for Mimes, Clowns, Jugglers, and Puppetteers," P. O. Box 453, Times Square Station, New York, NY 10108.

Movies

"A Clown is Born," "The Mark of the Clown," "That's Life." These are marketed through Mass Media Ministries, 2116 North Charles St., Baltimore, MD 21218.

Major Makeup Companies

(Write these companies for catalogs of their makeup products. Some of the companies have a list of distributors which they will also send you. For local sources check in the yellow pages of the telephone directory. Look under these headings: Stage Makeup, Theatrical Makeup, Theatrical Supplies, Makeup (theatrical), Costume and Makeup.

Bob Kelly Cosmetics, Inc., 151 West 46th Street, New York, NY 10036.

Kryolan (manufactured in Germany). Order through Alcone Co., Inc., 575 Eighth Ave., New York, NY 10018.

Max Factor Makeup Studios, 6922 Hollywood Blvd., Hollywood, CA 90028.

Mehron, Inc., 250 W. 40th St., New York, NY 10018.

Ben Nye Company, Inc., 11571 Santa Monica Blvd., Los Angeles, CA 90025.

Paramount Theatrical Supplies, 575 Eighth Ave., New York, NY 10018. (Also the Alcone Co.)

Stein Cosmetic Co., 430 Broome Street, New York, NY 10013.

Organizations and Conferences

"Clown, Mime, Puppet, and Dance Workshops," P. O. Box 24023, Nashville, TN 37202.

Clowns of America, Inc. P. O. Box 3906, Baltimore, MD 21222. (Publisher of *Calliope* Magazine.)

"Drama Leadership Conference" (National Clowning, Puppetry, and Drama conference held at Ridgecrest, NC). For information write Drama Specialist, Baptist Sunday School Board, Nashville, TN 37234.

Faith and Fantasy (National clown ministry organization founded by Floyd Shaffer). For information write to 32185 Susilane, Roseville, MI 48066.

Holy Fools (National clown ministry organization founded by Bill Peckham). For information write at P. O. Box 1828, Springfield, IL 62701.

"National Clowning Seminar" (Held in March each year in Nashville, TN). For information write Church Program Training Center, Baptist Sunday School Board, Nashville, TN 37234.

Special Clown Resource Companies and Organizations

Church Recreation Department, Baptist Sunday School Board, Nashville, TN 37234. (How-to information, routines, and scripts.)

The Circus Clowns, 2835 Nicollet Ave., Minneapolis, MN 55408. (Complete line of clowning materials.)

Contemporary Drama Service, Box 457-WZ, Downers Grove, IL 60515. (How-to kits, routines, and scripts.)

Funny Farm Clowns, Inc., Route 2, Butler, GA 31006. (Complete line of clowning materials.)

Griffin Shoe Company, P. O. Box 7601, Rochester, NY 14622. (Oversize clown shoes.)

Habits Magic Manufacturing Company, Cologne, MI 49040. (Write for a catalog of clown magic resources.)

Ringling Clown College, P. O. Box 1528, Venice, FL 33595. (General clowning information: makeup, routines, etc.)

Bibliography

Bibliography

Bingo's Makeup Notes. The Circus Clowns. Minneapolis, MN.

Bishop, George. *The World of Clowns.* Brooke House Pub., Los Angeles, CA, 1976.

Blankenship, Mark, compiler and arranger. *Singing Is Fun.* Broadman Press, Nashville, TN, 1978. (Book, cassette tape, and record available.)

Blankenship, Mark, compiler and arranger. *Singing Is Fun* (vol 2). Broadman Press, Nashville, TN, 1981. (Book, split track tapes, and record available.)

Burgess, Hovey. *Circus Techniques.* Thomas Y. Crowell Co., Pub., New York, 1977.

Bursill, Henry. *Hand Shadows.* Dover Publications, New York.

The Complete Floyd Shaffer Clown Ministry Workshop Kit, Dennis C. Benson, P. O. Box 12811, Pittsburgh, PA 15241.

Davis, Jimmy. *One Balloon Zoo.* Magic Inc., Chicago, IL 60625.

Denard, Harold. *How To Do Rope Tricks.* Magic Inc., Chicago, IL (6th printing), 1979.

Dewey, Ralph. *Basic Balloon Sculpturing Course.* Dewey, 1110 E. Princeton, Deer Park, TX 77536.

Dewey, Ralph. *Dewey's Balloon and Clown Notebook.*

Dewey, Ralph. *Dewey's Gospel Balloon Routines #1.*

Dewey, Ralph. *Dewey's New Balloon Animals.*

Dewey, Ralph. *Dewey's Bubble Buddies.*

Disher, M. Willson, *Clowns and Pantomimes.* Benjamin Blom Pub., New York, 1968.

Ferrell, Tom, and Eisenberg, Lee. *Sneaky Feats: The Art of Showing Off and 53 Ways to Do It.* Sneed and Ward Pub., Kansas City, 1975.

Fluegelman, Andrew, ed. *The New Games Book.* New York: Doubleday, 1976.

Gibson, Walter B. *The New Magician's Manual.* Dover Pub., New York.

Hamblin, Kay. *Mime: A Playbook of Silent Fantasy.* Doubleday Pub., New York, 1978.

Hartish, Karl. *Introduction to Clowning.* Clowns of America, Baltimore, MD, 1973.

Holden, Max. *Manual of Juggling.* Magic Inc., Chicago, IL (5th printing), 1979.

Hornby, John. *Clowns Through the Ages.* The Byways Library, Henry Z. Walck, Inc., 1962.

How to Make Your Own Clown Face. Ringling Bros. Barnum and Bailey Circus, P. O. Box 1528, Venice, FL 33595.

James, Stewart. *Abbott's Encyclopedia of Rope Tricks.* Dover Pub., New York, 10014.

Jayne, Caroline Furness. *String Figures and How to Make Them.* Dover Pub., New York, 1962.

Kerns, Ernie. *How to be a Magic Clown* #1 and #2. Magic Inc., Chicago, IL, 1973, 1974.

Kipnis, Claude. *The Mime Book.* Harper and Row Pub., New York, 1974.

Liebig, Ernie and Jean. *Clowning Is . . .*, Bullard, TX.

McVicar, Wes. *Clown Omnibus.* Association Press, New York.

Murray, Marion. *Circus.* Appleton-Century-Crofts, Inc. Pub., New York, 1956.

Pearce, Richard. *Stages of the Clown.* Southern Illinois University Press, Carbondale, IL, 1970.

Robertson, Everett. *Using Puppetry in the Church.* Broadman Press, Nashville, TN, 1976.

Robertson, Everett. *Introduction to Church Drama.* Convention Press, Nashville, TN, 1978.

Sanders, Toby. *How to Be a Complete Clown.* Stein and Day Pub., New York, 1978.

Schindler, George. *Magic with Everyday Objects.* Stein and Day Pub., New York, 1976 (rev. 1980).

Seigel, Roger. *Rubber Ark.* Magic Inc., Chicago, IL 60625.

Stoenberg, Mark. *Clowns for Circus and Stage.* Sterling Pub. & Co., New York, 1981.

Toll, Robert C. *On with the Show.* Oxford University Press, New York, 1976.

Williams, Margery. *The Velveteen Rabbit.* Doubleday, New York.